DATE			

THE
PHOENIX
FACTOR

THE
PHOENIX
FACTOR

Surviving and Growing
Through Personal Crisis

DR. KARL SLAIKEU

AND

STEVE LAWHEAD

HOUGHTON MIFFLIN COMPANY/BOSTON/1985

Library of Congress Cataloging in Publication Data
Slaikeu, Karl A., date
  The phoenix factor.
  Bibliography: p.
  1. Crisis intervention (Psychiatry)   I. Lawhead,
Steve. II. Title.
RC480.6.S55 1985   158'.1   85-4254
ISBN 0-395-35405-6

Printed in the United States of America

Q 10 9 8 7 6 5 4 3 2 1

In all of the case histories in this book the authors
have used fictitious names and traits not identifiable as
those of any particular person.

Book design by Victoria Hartman

The authors are grateful for permission to quote as follows: For the list of various distorted
beliefs reprinted on pages 108–10, taken from *Multidimensional Psychotherapy: A Counselors'
Guide for the MAP Form*, by D. C. Hammond and K. Stanfield, copyright © 1976, 1977, by
the Institute for Personality and Ability Testing, Inc. Reprinted by permission. For the "Dear
Abby" letter quoted on pages 113–14, taken from the "Dear Abby" column. Copyright, 1985,
Universal Press Syndicate. Reprinted with permission. All rights reserved. For the "Life
Events Checklist" on pages 120–21 from "The Social Readjustment Rating Scale," by T. H.
Holmes and R. H. Rahe, reprinted with permission from *Journal of Psychosomatic Research*, v.
11, Pergamon Press, Ltd. For "The Stages of Crisis" on page 207, with permission from The
Charles Press, Publishers, Philadelphia, Pennsylvania. For the "Developmental Table" on
pages 217–22 and "Situational Crises" table on pages 225–26, from Karl A. Slaikeu, *Crisis
Intervention: A Handbook for Practice and Research*. Copyright © 1984 by Allyn and Bacon,
Inc. Reprinted with permission.

To Margaret Erickson Slaikeu
— who has truly grown through crisis

Contents

Preface

THIS BOOK represents an unusual collaborative effort: a psychologist and a writer of fantasy and science fiction teaming up for a book on how to overcome personal crisis.

It all began with the psychologist telling the SF writer about what it was like to work with people in crisis — how even the most severe and devastating personal crises held enormous potential for good. Indeed, the destruction of the old life actually had within it the seeds of a new — and often better — life.

The SF writer asked to hear more and was told about the research done with survivors of crisis. Survivors more than merely "survived"; through taking care of their bodies, managing painful feelings, changing attitudes, and adjusting their behavior, they found ways to renew themselves.

"That's the Phoenix!" said the SF writer. "New life out of ashes."

And so it is.

We wrote this book as if we were talking to one of Dr. Slaikeu's clients, or to anyone who has been devastated by a major life crisis — the death of a loved one, the loss of an important relationship, a financial setback, serious illness, traumatic injury, or any of a host of personal catastrophes.

It doesn't have to be a recent event. Many of our readers, like those who seek professional help, are suffering from wounds inflicted years ago by some crisis that was never resolved. Whether recent or long past, however, you'll find right away that we aim for more than simple repair or recovery. Crisis theory points to a remarkable fact of human growth and development: newer, more satisfying, and more productive ways of living can come about only *after* the old ways have died.

It has often been quite difficult for us to put this psychological truth into words in such a way that it doesn't come across as blatantly offensive to someone who is suffering the trauma of a crisis. Most of us don't want "growth" — we want . . . our daughter to be alive again, our spouse to return home, our boss to give us another chance, the doctor to say that he's made a mistake.

In other words, we want what we've lost, not something new — no matter how appealing.

Each reader, depending upon his or her situation, will use this book in a different way. If you're in pain right now, not knowing where to turn next, start with Chapter One and move right through to Chapter Three, "Giving Yourself Psychological First Aid."

If your situation is less urgent, then you may want to take more time with each chapter, even spread the reading out over a number of months. Chapter Four, "A Blueprint for Growth," will tell you where we're headed. The rest of the book is actually a detailed version of the ideas presented in that chapter.

Whatever your situation, however you use this book, remember that the principles discussed in each chapter apply to you. We firmly believe that every crisis, no matter what it is, presents unique opportunities for growth, for change, for new and better life. If you are hurting, trying to cope with perhaps the worst ordeal you have ever experienced, this book is for you.

*

We are indebted to numerous people for their contributions to the development of this book. Doctors Coval MacDonald and Steve Tulkin each read the manuscript in its early stages and provided helpful critique. Jane Stewart and Becky Nystrom typed several drafts and helped by cross-checking references. We are also grateful to our editor at Houghton Mifflin, Ruth Hapgood, for her enthusiasm and insight, and to Lois Randall, manuscript editor, for her careful attention to detail. We are especially thankful to Sandy Hintz, our literary agent, for finding a home for our book at Houghton Mifflin. Finally, our thanks to our wives, Diane W. Slaikeu and Alice S. Lawhead, who offered unflagging support and more constructive suggestions than we had a right to expect.

Karl A. Slaikeu, Ph.D.
Steve Lawhead
January 1985

THE
PHOENIX
FACTOR

· ONE ·

Danger and Opportunity

THE HEADLINES are full of bad news:

Young Woman Raped in Washroom
Jet Airliner Crashes on Takeoff
Unemployment Figures Up
Divorce Takes Toll on Children
Fire Destroys Apartment Building
Terrorists Take Hostages
Hurricane Death Toll Reaches 65
Murder Rate Linked to Joblessness
Skyway Collapses onto Crowded Dance Floor
Suicide on the Increase
Cancer Claims One in Four Americans
Nuclear Waste Leak Threatens City

The never-ending stream of words and pictures on the front page tells a story of crisis. The world is in crisis. Inevitably, our lives are touched by the crisis events around us. There is no escape.

To be alive and to be human is to know crisis. No one is immune. Whether through severe illness, the death of a loved one, loss of a job, serious accident, or some other traumatic experience, we all realize sooner or later that we are not invulnerable, that "accidents" don't just happen to the other guy.

Somewhere, sometime, in some way you will face a crisis.

Or maybe you already have. If so, you know the terrible upheaval, the helplessness, the hopelessness, the fear and hurt and anger. If you have lived through a crisis, you know how it feels and what it can do to you.

You can't eat. You can't sleep. Your stomach is tied up in knots, queasy; you want to vomit. You can't talk. You cry. You are nervous, jittery, on edge. You are afraid. Bitter. Confused.

You ask: Why me? What did I do? Why is this happening? What is wrong with me? What will my friends think? What am I going to do? How will I survive? Will my life ever be the same again?

In crisis, the very fabric of your life is ripped apart under powerful forces beyond your control. This is the bad news of a crisis. But there is good news, too.

THE PHOENIX FACTOR

As bad as it is, as terrible as it makes you feel, a crisis can be survived. What is more, a time of crisis can be turned into a time of growth.

A crisis does not have to end in total loss. A crisis can become a means of achieving greater personal enrichment. A crisis can be conquered.

The Chinese picture symbol for the word *crisis* indicates both *danger* and *opportunity*. The danger of loss and hurt and the opportunity for gain and health. The ancients realized that in times of great upheaval, when the stakes are very high and the outcome much in doubt, then the possibility exists for creating something new and better. Out of the chaos can come a new and better order.

This hopeful feature of crisis is what we call the Phoenix Factor. The phoenix of mythology was a wondrous bird that lived for a thousand years and died in a sudden burst of flame. As its funeral pyre burned, the phoenix underwent a magical transformation — instead of being consumed, the phoenix rose from the flames, born anew, more beautiful than ever, to live another thousand years.

There is a phoenix factor in human life, too. When your world collapses in the flames of crisis, you can emerge reborn. Beauty can rise from the ashes. And thus a crisis can be seen as a turning point — the place where your life teeters on the brink of the unknown. True, a crisis can lead to disaster, but it can also lead to rebirth, to greater growth. What makes the difference between a crisis that results in immediate harm or subsequent psychological problems and a crisis that leads to rebirth, growth, and maturity?

The difference is in knowing how to turn the crisis to your advantage, to take control of the event and channel it into a course toward growth. The phoenix factor is present in every crisis situation, but you have to know how to use it.

Not only can it be done; you can do it. Perhaps not simply or painlessly, but with proper understanding of the nature of crisis and knowledge of the techniques explained in this book, you can turn crisis away from harm and toward health. Like the phoenix of old, you can rise to live again, stronger, more mature, more in control of your life than you ever believed possible.

· TWO ·

Anatomy of a Crisis

FOR BILL AND HELEN the day began normally enough. They woke to the alarm and Helen roused the kids for school while Bill showered and dressed for work. After a noisy breakfast, Helen distributed lunch boxes and pushed her brood out the door with the usual admonitions to be careful and to watch out for cars on the way to school. Then she settled back for a quiet moment and a cup of coffee before beginning the day's chores.

As she finished her last sip the phone rang. She answered and was informed that there had been an accident on the playground, and that five-year-old Tammy had been rushed to the hospital. Helen was told to go to the emergency room at once. The school official could tell her nothing more.

In an anguished frenzy Helen rushed to the hospital, where she found Bill waiting, gray-faced and nervous. "What is it, Bill? What has happened to Tammy?"

"I don't know. They won't tell me anything."

Just then a tall young doctor approached with the terrible news. "I am sorry," he said. "Your daughter has died of head injuries sustained in an accident on the playground this morning. There was nothing we could do. I'm terribly sorry."

THE CRISIS BOMB

A crisis is a bomb that explodes in your life and shatters it. More specifically, a crisis is a state of extreme emotional upset that is touched off by some hazardous event. The tremendous upheaval, hurt, and despair do not just materialize out of thin air; they are caused by a specific experience, whether it be the death of a loved one, getting fired from a job, finding out you have cancer, or moving from your home in South Carolina to North Dakota.

Some events are so universally devastating that they almost always set off a crisis. The death of a child, for example.

Other experiences are more subtle. In and of itself the event might be a relatively small affair. But since it comes on the top of a number of other stressful events it touches off a crisis.

Bob, aged thirty-nine, was having a rough time at home. His wife had been complaining that he was spending too much time at work and too little time with the family — especially with Michael, who was not doing well in school. Financial pressures, however, had made it nearly impossible for him to work less. He had come to depend on the overtime hours just to make ends meet.

One morning Bob received a call from his son's principal. "I'd like you to come see me as soon as possible," said the principal. "Michael has been skipping classes for weeks. I think we need to discuss it, or we will have to suspend him."

That same afternoon Bob was called into his supervisor's office and informed that the promotion he had been expecting for some time and that he had hoped would make things easier on him, would not be taking place. "The company," he was told, "has decided to bring in a man from another department."

That night Bob went home early. He was very quiet at dinner and throughout the evening. Just before bed his wife found him in the bathroom weeping and saying that his life was over. His dreams had come to an end.

THE LAST STRAW

Quite often the crisis event is described as the "last straw" — that seemingly insignificant happening that signals the final collapse. Being passed over for a promotion, for example, would not normally set off a crisis. But following on the heels of marital difficulty, financial pressures, a child doing poorly in school, and the bitter disappointment of losing part of a life's dream, the promotion incident set the fuse that ignited the crisis.

Whether distinguished by its suddenness and severity (rape, unexpected death, natural disaster) or by its subtlety (observing one's fortieth birthday, moving to a new city, changing jobs), one feature of a crisis is that is arises directly out of some event or happening in your life.

THINKING MAKES IT SO

Crisis events can fall into one of three categories:

An event can be a *loss* of something or someone. If my son dies, or my wife leaves me, the physical losses are apparent. Loss can also be of self-esteem, or of a lifelong dream, or of some other intangible possession.

An event can be a *threat* to the established order of our lives. Getting fired from an important job might threaten to swamp a lifestyle accustomed to indulging expensive tastes and could bring about a crisis.

An event can present a *challenge* for which we are unprepared in some way. This accounts for the fact that seemingly positive events can also contain crisis potential.

*

Sally, a teller in a bank, was very good at her job. So good, in fact, that she was made manager over the other tellers at her branch. She liked her new job but soon began to have doubts about it. She no longer ate lunch with her friends at work, feeling uncomfortable around them because she often had to give negative feedback to her tellers — women who had been her peers. Sally was now the "boss" and was expected to fire tellers who could not keep up with the job's demands.

Weeks passed and she became irritable, complaining that the money wasn't worth it. Her work suffered. At home she couldn't eat, and sometimes would wake up at night for no reason and could not get back to sleep. She began taking sick leave regularly and eventually decided to quit her job for another somewhere else. Once she had left the bank, however, she did not actively look for another job, preferring instead to stay at home and watch TV.

Sally had been confronted with a challenge that she was unwilling or unable to accept. It threatened the image she had of herself as a competent worker. Her promotion required a reorganization of her life, using new skills, handling new responsibilities, making decisions, and managing others. She was unwilling to take the risk that the new job presented to her.

In understanding a crisis you must look beyond the event itself to see what the event means to you, to determine how you perceive it. Is it a threat? Does it represent a loss? A challenge you are unready to accept at this time?

The promotion experiences for Sally and for Bob violated certain expectations they had about their lives. Bob saw that his denied promotion was a threat to his dream. Sally's promotion, on the other hand, was a challenge she did not feel able to accept. For Bill and Helen, Tammy's death was a sudden and devastating loss. They couldn't bear the thought of her suffering in the accident, nor could they imagine life without her.

I CAN'T COPE

A crisis event — like a bomb going off in your life — demands that you do something to cope with the situation. But your inability to cope using customary methods is what makes it a crisis — instead of simply a problem or an upsetting experience.

When Tammy died in the playground accident Helen was so overcome with grief that she could no longer handle the normal routine of her day. She could not bring herself to prepare the family's meals, go out shopping, or clean the house. She would not speak to her friends or greet her neighbors. For Bill, concentrating on his work became a chore; he felt tired and despondent. His ulcer started acting up again, and time after time he found himself shouting angrily at the other children for little or no reason at all.

An experience brings about a crisis when it so overwhelms your normal problem-solving and coping methods that they break down under the strain. When the old ways of handling difficulty — such as taking a walk, going to a movie, talking to a friend, yelling at the dog, taking a vacation, or whatever — no longer work, you are in a crisis.

In fact, the failure of normal coping methods in the face of this new and overpowering situation is what separates a crisis from some other kind of life problem. If you could handle the upset, talk about your feelings, think through the problem, then it wouldn't be a crisis. We might say you were having a very rough time, perhaps, but not a crisis.

A crisis brings with it intense and bewildering emotions — guilt, fear, resentment, rage, despair, even hate. It dwarfs all attempts to comprehend the situation, and it opens the door for all kinds of erratic behavior.

I'M GOING CRAZY

George received the shocking news that his father had been killed under mysterious circumstances. His father's bullet-riddled body had been found in the trunk of a stolen car on a lonely stretch of road outside the city. No one had a clue as to why George's father had been a victim in such a brutal slaying.

George took the news calmly at first. As the eldest in his family he took care of all the funeral arrangements and comforted the others in the family through the ordeal. One month later, while moving his deceased father's furniture into storage in his basement, he tripped on the stairs and broke his arm.

Breaking his arm was the last straw for George. Normally an easygoing guy, he complained constantly about the pain and started taking pain pills for his arm — sometimes taking more pills than prescribed. He began waking up at night and walking aimlessly around the house, haunted by visions of his father's brutal death. He refused to enter his workshop in the basement, where he normally spent many happy hours puttering around.

One night he confided to his wife that he feared he was going crazy. He believed he could feel his sanity slipping away.

The tremendous upheaval of a crisis touches every area of life. It unleashes new emotions, dramatically upsets the normal routine, produces physical symptoms or illnesses, creates friction in relationships with others, and profoundly affects the normal view of self and life.

Most people in crisis describe themselves as feeling as though they are going crazy; they are surprised by their own reactions. They may be angrier than they have ever been before or find themselves crying uncontrollably when they had taken bad news pretty smoothly in the past. They have thoughts they never had before — of hurting themselves, or hurting others, or running away to a foreign country. They do things they have never done before — like lashing out at a family member or telling their boss to go to hell.

Actually, these are normal reactions to abnormal events.

The fact that a man whose father was murdered finds himself unable to sleep at night, and worrying about it, simply means that he is in touch with the realities around him.

A proper paraphrase of Kipling's poem "If" might be: "If you can keep your head while all about you are losing theirs . . . then you don't understand the situation."

You should expect disorganization, emotional flare-ups, unusual behavior, and feelings of helplessness and confusion. These are normal reactions to the severe trauma of a crisis. The trick, as we shall see later in this book, is learning how to manage the feelings and to control the erratic behavior, until life evens out once more.

I'M FALLING APART!

Tom was a blunt, heavy-handed construction worker with definite ideas about a woman's place in the world. He arrived home one night to find a note from his wife saying that she had left him for another man. Bewildered, he read the note over and over and looked around the apartment. All her things were gone. She had indeed moved out.

For three days he acted as if nothing were wrong. He went to work as usual, but at night he cruised the bars talking to his drinking buddies about how unreliable women were. Finally, he confided to his closest friend that his wife, Jean, had left him. With that admission he broke down and began to cry. He had never cried over anything in his adult life, and the tears scared him more than he could say. He kept repeating over and over, "I'm falling apart . . . I'm not going to make it. Somebody help me! I'm falling apart!"

The horrible feeling that control of your life is slipping away is a definite feature of a crisis. You have sustained a terrible blow that has left you defenseless. You are vulnerable, perhaps in a way you never have been before. You feel this vulnerability acutely — it feels as if there is nothing holding you together anymore.

This time of vulnerability is a time of danger, but also a time ripe with opportunity. When you can't cope, when your defenses are down, when you are at a loss about how to handle the situation, you are suddenly open to any means to get through the experience. The slightest push one way or the other — an idea, a friend's statement, a change in outlook — can tilt you toward growth or toward harm.

In the above example, Tom found himself helpless and vulnerable. His wife's leaving jolted him so much that for the first time in his life he was ready to hear a new truth about himself. The crisis brought him to a place where he could be open to alternatives.

Vulnerability opens the door for new and different ideas. This is the supreme opportunity for growth to begin.

WILL IT EVER END?

A crisis does not last forever. Though the consequences of a crisis can remain a lifetime, the extreme upset and disorganization does not last. You can't cry forever, rant and rave forever, quit eating forever.

No matter what caused the crisis — death of a loved one, marital problems, physical injury, rape — the extreme terror, hurt, and panic go away in a few weeks or months. The human body will not allow us to stay in a state of extreme pain any longer than necessary. We naturally "put ourselves back together" again one way or another.

Here's the rub. In what way do we put ourselves back together? Do we reorganize our lives in a way that will be good for us in the years to come? Or do we reconstruct our lives in a way that closes us off to better options in living, restricts relationships, and insures a negative, pessimistic outlook on life?

THREE POSSIBLE OUTCOMES

When his wife left him, Tom's life collapsed. He had stomachaches, and the crying incident was repeated often in the weeks to come, usually when he was alone at night.

But after a while his stomach quit bothering him. He no longer cried when he thought about his wife and the other man. His friends said that he was his old self again.

Tom was not his "old self" again. He had changed dramatically. The new Tom was profoundly unhappy and lonely. Though stability had re-emerged in his life, it was based on his solemn vow "never to trust a woman again."

People do not emerge from a crisis unchanged. The crisis is resolved in one of three ways: death, debility, or growth.

Newspapers are filled with accounts of suicide (and occasional suicide/homicide situations) that occur close on the heels of a life crisis. Some traumatic experiences so overwhelm the individual that he or she simply cannot bear the thought of going on. The end of life is an all-too-real possibility in many crisis situations.

More often, however, the crisis ends in debility — weakness, hurt, long-term psychological harm.

Debility
Susan had taught school for many years. She enjoyed her remedial classes, but was concerned to see a gradual change in

attitude among many of her newer students. They seemed to come to class solely to bully her and to challenge her authority. She even began receiving threats from some of the more belligerent students.

When the attack came she did not expect it: a magazine rolled around a pipe slammed full force into her neck as she stood at the blackboard with her back to the class. It knocked her down, but she got up and taught her two remaining classes that day. Then she went home . . . to stay.

Susan never returned to her classroom. She says she hasn't gone back because her neck injury causes her acute headaches and dizziness. She also says she's afraid.

"I'm petrified when I see more than two youngsters together. If I want to go out in the evening, I have to work up my courage all day." Susan, a tenured professional, needs only to complete her dissertation to earn a doctoral degree. Yet she still dissolves into tears whenever she thinks about the incident. "I know I'm not handling this very well," she says. "It's been two years and I'm getting worse. I'm very bitter."

Many people never seem to get past the crisis. Like Susan, they are continually haunted by the terrible memory of what happened. They never seem to get over the bitterness, anger, hurt, or remorse. They cannot function at their jobs, their relationships break down, and their mental abilities slip as well.

Death
In the year following his son's death from leukemia, Jim had become a very lonely and bitter man. He withdrew into himself further and further, so estranging himself from his wife that they became divorced. Alone, he stayed awake for long periods — sometimes two or three days in a row — just thinking about what had happened.

Finally, on the day of the first anniversary of his son's death, Jim calmly walked into the hospital where his little boy had been cared for, brought out a rifle he had hidden in his coat, and took his son's doctors hostage at gunpoint. The incident ended thirty-two hours later when police, fearing for the hostages, rushed him. Jim was wounded in the ensuing gunfire and died moments later.

Jim clearly had not worked through the crisis of his son's death — a loss he could not get over. The aftermath of the crisis had touched every area of his life and had left him unable to function normally. Jim's actions were those of a desperate, hurting man.

Growing Through a Crisis

The third possible outcome of a crisis is growth. That can mean many things, including increased coping skills, broader and more mature attitudes about life, improved interpersonal relationships, enhanced self-awareness, greater independence and openness to new experiences, greater sensitivity to the needs and problems of others, stronger ties with loved ones, increased ability to deal with life's problems in constructive ways.

Growth is the only positive outcome of a crisis.

Whatever form it takes, growth may be defined as working through the crisis experience so that it becomes a part of the fabric of life, leaving you open and ready to face the future. You have experienced growth as a result of a crisis if, when it is over, you are ready to resume the business of living, working, playing, and loving.

Often, people who have grown through a crisis talk about the fact that they discovered new skills and resources they had never known before — the same way people often point to the fact that getting fired from one job ultimately propelled them into a vocation they had dreamed about all their lives.

Many people describe becoming more in touch with their feelings. Men, especially, become more tender and expressive of their emotions, more gentle with their spouses, more caring, more loving, as a result of having been jolted by a marital crisis.

Some crises bring families closer together. Often it is only by experiencing the depths of tragic loss that family members realize how much they mean to each other. Growth takes place when they learn to express their caring more openly to one another.

New dreams, new plans, new attitudes about life, can open up to people who have successfully resolved serious crises. Many find new meaning in previously dormant religious beliefs, developing more mature, more adult understandings of God. In some of the more startling testimonials in religious literature people describe how they were able to cast off outdated, antiquated, or meaningless beliefs for a real and relevant faith, only after having gone through a very traumatic experience. Many people come to see themselves as stronger than they ever thought they could be; they form a healthier self-image.

Growth as a result of a crisis can occur in every area of life. However, the stakes are very high. There is danger here as well as opportunity.

NEW LIFE FROM THE ASHES

In the following chapters we will explore the phoenix factor and find what it means to grow through a crisis. We will show you how to turn personal crisis away from harm and toward growth, using proven strategies of crisis resolution. The phoenix factor is not magic, nor is it based on luck or chance. The phoenix factor is actually a blueprint for growth that can be used in the days, weeks, months, and even years following any crisis event.

The early days of crisis require special measures and precautions, which we outline in the next chapter. Growth is furthest from your mind when everything is coming down on you at once. Getting through it any way you can is what counts most, which may even mean coping with threats of suicide or homicide.

But growth is more than simply staying afloat, or warding off destruction. Chapter Four, "A Blueprint for Growth," describes four steps that you can take to grow through your crisis in the months and years ahead. New life can come from the ashes and ruin of loss, but it doesn't come automatically. Chapters Five to Ten ease you into the idea of growth and wrap up with very concrete ways to change not only attitudes but also your everyday behavior in order to live in the future.

Chapter Twelve summarizes the principles we've discussed and answers some frequently asked questions about our method. The Appendixes offer even more detail on the types of crises you may face, as well as advice on how to find outside help if necessary.

At the heart of the phoenix factor is the idea that the pain of crisis can be turned to your advantage. You already know that your life will never be the same. What you may not know is how to direct your efforts to open up a new, and even better, future for yourself.

While change is often a painful process, it also brings rewards that at first may be hidden. By following the suggestions in this book you can grow in ways you may never have thought possible. Others have done it; so can you.

THREE

Giving Yourself Psychological First Aid

THE FIRST FEW DAYS and weeks of a crisis can be the most difficult. You can be overwhelmed by painful feelings, terrifying thoughts, and perhaps a whole range of nagging physical complaints, too. You may not know where to turn or what to do next, though you may feel the need to do *something* right away.

It is normal, in the heat of a crisis, to want to handle all your problems at once. A woman whose husband leaves her is suddenly confronted with a flood of questions, each demanding an immediate answer:

> Why did he do it?
> Is it a reflection on me?
> Will I be alone from now on?
> Will he come back?
> What will my friends think?
> Will this hurt the children?
> What should I tell them tonight?
> Should I go ahead with the party next week?
> Should I go to church alone on Sunday?
> Did he leave me for another woman?
> What is she like?
> Should I try to talk to her?

This flood of questions, thoughts, and feelings is normal, but since there is no way to deal with everything all at once you must choose what to take care of right now and what to postpone until later.

Doctors working in hospital emergency rooms are frequently faced with situations that demand they make priority decisions. The victim of an accident may have numerous injuries — some more serious than others. They cannot all be treated at once, so the doctor decides which must be treated promptly and which can wait until later. Therapists and counselors also recognize a distinction between psychological first aid and crisis therapy.

The goal of psychological first aid is simply to bind the wounds, so to speak, to help you take the first necessary steps toward coping. One of the characteristics of a crisis is that your customary problem-solving methods have broken down. A whole range of disruptive thoughts and feelings — anger, shock, pain, depression — confuse and overwhelm your coping systems. Psychological first aid is designed to help you deal with the disruptive thoughts and feelings so that normal problem solving can begin right now.

Crisis therapy, on the other hand, is something completely different. Its goals are much more ambitious and take longer to achieve. Crisis therapy is designed to help you work through the crisis in such a way that the traumatic event becomes woven into the overall fabric of your life, taking its place beside the other events of your life and leaving you ready to face the future. This can take many months, and sometimes years, to complete fully because the activities of crisis therapy are spread out over many weeks and months.

When a crisis first strikes, what you need is psychological first aid — just as the accident victim needs physical first aid in the emergency room. You do not need long-range crisis therapy; that would not help you very much right now. Instead, you need a way to help you decide what must be done now and what can wait until later.

This chapter will help you give yourself psychological first aid. Your concern about the future, your questions about how everything is going to turn out, can wait for the moment.

Right now you must simply concentrate on staying alive, keeping your options open, reducing your losses, just living through this day so that you can begin another one tomorrow.

In the chapters to follow we will talk about growth and how to discover the opportunity that is present in even very dangerous and stressful crisis situations. For now, however, let survival be your only goal.

ALLOW YOURSELF TO FEEL BAD

Now is a good time to remind yourself that life will not be business as usual for a while. In fact, it would be best if you did not even try to be "normal."

Many people actually compound their problems by imposing their usual standards on themselves and then feel guilty because they can't make themselves feel as good as they usually do. A crisis, however, is not a normal time. A crisis, by definition, is a time when everything is abnormal.

While Will's older brothers moved away to take jobs in the city, Will stayed on the farm to help his father. He wanted nothing more than to be a farmer and to work the land that his father and grandfather had worked. He enrolled in a college nearby to study agriculture so that he would be the best farmer he could be.

Will got his chance a lot sooner than he ever expected when, one day toward the end of his freshman year, his dad fainted in the field. Will was able to get him to the emergency room at the hospital in town, where his father was treated. The doctor told Will that his father had suffered a severe stroke and would likely be paralyzed the rest of his life.

Will quit school and assumed responsibility for the farm, working hard and long hours in an effort to keep up with all the chores; but with harvest time — the busiest season of the year — so close, there was so much to do that he fell further behind. Will became depressed over his inability to take care of the farm the way he wanted to; and making matters worse, his father, now at home, needed constant attention and criticized Will's every move.

In order to escape his father's criticism, Will began skipping meals and working far into the night; when he finally tumbled into bed weak with exhaustion he cried himself to sleep. Sometimes he had nightmares about the crops burning up in the fields while he just sat idly by and watched. He resented his father for leaving him with all the work and for not allowing him to become better prepared. He began thinking it would have been better if his father had died; then he felt guilty for having such terrible thoughts about his crippled father.

Will thought he was going crazy — he had no other explanation for his nightmares, tears, and guilt. In desperation, he sought a counselor and told him what had happened.

The counselor listened to Will's story and commented, "You know, Will, it's understandable that you would be so upset, considering all the changes taking place right now. Your life has been thrown into a tailspin. I think it's normal to feel upset at a time like this."

"Normal" — that was a comforting word for Will. He had not for a moment considered that what he might be feeling could be called normal. He had been resisting the stress of the situation, but it had been working on him just the same. With the counselor's help, however, Will began to see that it was all right to feel bad, to feel scared and helpless — bad feelings were normal in a bad situation.

Remember that your tears, anger, frustration, inability to eat or sleep, poor concentration, isolation from others — all these things are normal reactions to abnormal circumstances. The very fact that you are so distraught is your body's way of telling you that something is very wrong.

Therefore, give yourself permission to feel bad. Allow yourself to feel terrible. Be gentle with yourself. Remind yourself that you can only do what is required right now and that is enough.

The goal of first aid is survival. If you are reading this page, you are surviving, so give yourself credit for having come this far, and for putting yourself in a position to begin taking the first steps toward growth.

PROTECTING AGAINST FATAL MOVES

Perhaps you are wondering, "What's the use? Why should I go on?" Maybe you can't even conceive that things will get better, that life will ever feel good again, that there is a future for you. You may have times when you think, "It's all over for me. I might as well just give up."

You are not alone in thinking and feeling this way. One time or another, most people in crisis hit bottom and feel like giving up. Life looks so bleak that all sorts of fearful thoughts crowd in — thoughts that, if focused on exclusively, become immobilizing. Such as:

I can't go on! You may feel very small and insignificant in the face of such overwhelming adversity. You feel completely powerless, helpless, defenseless. You find yourself thinking over and over again that there is simply no use in trying to go on.

I can't handle this! You may see your situation as one that somebody else might be able to deal with, but not you. You say to yourself, "I am not strong enough to deal with this."

Or "I just don't have it in me. I don't have what it takes to get through this."

Nothing I do will make any difference! You may think that anything you might do to help yourself will ultimately fail. You think that if you try a new technique or get by for a day or two it won't last; eventually you'll end up at the bottom again and nothing will have changed. You feel doomed.

All of these thoughts and others like them are *immobilizers* — thoughts and feelings that stop you from acting, freeze your will to survive. They tell you there is no hope, that all effort is futile. They are the thoughts that hit you when you're down, when circumstances are at their worst, when you are gripped with panic and despair.

Occasionally, this feeling of hopelessness leads to very de-structive thoughts and actions — including suicide and hom-icide. One of the most frightening aspects of a crisis is that very destructive thoughts and impulses can be unleashed.

Such thoughts and impulses are fairly common. After all, when the normal patterns of life are severely disrupted it may seem as if there is no reason to go on living. Your reason for living may have rested squarely on the style of life you had achieved for yourself. When it is taken away — through loss of a loved one, a broken relationship, a financial failure — you might question whether the future is worth waiting for.

In other situations you may be angry at someone who you feel has destroyed your world. Or you may be so upset and confused that you have very little control over your own threatening impulses. Unfortunately, such violent impulses often lead to destructive behavior. You can see it in the ac-counts of murder-suicides that appear in the newspapers: the estranged spouse who kills his partner and then turns the weapon on himself, or the recently terminated employee who returns to work to shoot the boss who fired him.

For whatever reason — lack of control, or the thought that life in the future is not worth living — these violent, life-threatening impulses should be taken seriously. You must recognize when the dangerous impulses surface, and then take steps to protect yourself and others against fatal moves — actions that reduce options altogether.

Hope When Everything Seems Hopeless

It is an indisputable fact — underscored by those who work with suicidal people — that suicidal impulses, like homicidal impulses, are usually short-lived. The desire to die or hurt someone else normally diminishes, frequently in a matter of hours, but usually in a matter of days. This is not to say that the same impulse may not recur. It may, but the point is that the desire to die or to end life is never total and irrevocable — it can reverse quickly.

Your goal, given this fact, is to postpone decisions about ending life — your own or someone else's — until you can get outside help and can profit from the assistance of a trained counselor or therapist.

Most people end up hurting themselves or somebody else because they see absolutely no hope for any change in the situation. They see no way to save face if they feel they have done something that grossly violates society's standards. Or they see no meaning in life, given a certain medical condition, or a lifestyle that has been changed by the absence of a partner.

Experience with people in crisis, however, indicates that with the proper help, and by following principles such as those outlined in this book, the dark and gloomy view of the present and future can often change dramatically. Here is hope when everything seems hopeless: hang in there, your feelings will change.

Signs of Danger

Most people who are thinking about hurting themselves or somebody else signal this intention in some way — either in something they say or something they do. *Verbal* signs of danger might include comments like the following:

"Life isn't worth living anyway, is it?"

"I can't go on anymore!"

"I have all of my affairs, except one, taken care of."

Or there might be threats on someone else's life, such as:

"You'll be sorry."

"You'll pay for this."

Many times such comments are obvious; other times they are oblique, and you must read between the lines.

There can also be *nonverbal* or behavioral danger signs — driving a car recklessly or overindulging in alcohol or other drugs, almost as if tempting fate.

Such statements and behavior must be taken seriously — especially when one or more of the following factors are present:

1. If you have made a plan to hurt yourself (or someone else), there is a greater chance of something bad happening. Buying a gun or saving pills in order to have a lethal dosage are common examples.

2. If you have a history of violent behavior (hitting other people, threatening them) or of suicide attempts that failed, you are more at risk than someone who has no such history.

3. If you are avoiding contact with others, you have increased the chances of harming yourself or someone else, since there will be no one around to stop you.

What to Do

Simply having thoughts of hurting yourself or somebody else does not automatically mean that you'll do it. But the thought in combination with one or more of the other ingredients listed above could well mean trouble. In other words, a threat, when combined with the opportunity to carry it out — buying weapons, securing pills, driving a car recklessly, consuming too much alcohol while feeling angry — indicates danger. The danger must be taken seriously, and the following steps should be taken:

1. Ask for help. Call a counselor, your minister/rabbi/ priest, or call a crisis hot line to talk over your problems, and ask for assistance. (See Appendix C, "Getting Outside Help.") You need help in sorting through the problem and deciding how to handle your destructive feelings.

2. Remove any weapons or other items that might allow you to carry out your destructive plans. The combination of weapons and your troublesome feelings could be lethal.

3. Remind yourself continually that your violent impulses will change — don't act on something now that will change later. Also, entertain the positive (reasons to live) as well as the negative (reasons to die or hurt someone) aspects of your situation. Keep all your options open until you have a chance to talk things over with a counselor.

For a Friend in Danger
Follow the same steps outlined above. If your friend needs to be in touch with outside help, express your concerns and tell your friend that you would like to get assistance. If the friend will not see a counselor willingly, then call the counselor or hot line yourself to ask for advice on how to deal with the troubled friend who won't take steps to insure proper care of him- or herself.

There are other steps you can take while waiting for help:

1. Ask your friend to talk about the situation. As the friend does so, draw him or her out on the various positive and neg- ative aspects — the desire to live, compared with the desire to die. This ambivalence, remember, is what the therapist will use in helping your friend to put off life-threatening behavior until that person has a chance to work through the problem.

2. Make a specific contract with your friend to stay in touch with you and to call you if things get really bad. It is important for people who are grappling with destructive thoughts to know that they are expected to contact someone if their outlook takes a turn for the worse.

Fighting Back

It is worth reminding yourself that everybody has black, hopeless thoughts during a crisis. The tendency, however, is to believe that you are somehow unique, that you are the only person to feel this way and think these depressing thoughts. You blame yourself for not being stronger, for not bouncing back, for not taking things in your stride.

The best antidote for depressing, immobilizing thoughts is to fight back. Attack them with truer, more balanced, more hopeful thoughts. When hopeless thoughts strike, tell yourself:

"Even though I may have no control over what happened, I do have control over how I will react to it." Your spouse, for example, may want to walk out. You can't control what she wants to do; you can't keep her from leaving. However, you do have certain choices — all the way from telling her to get out and helping her pack, to asking her to stay and talk things over, to calling a friend for help, to leaving yourself first!

How *you respond* to the crisis event is actually more important to survival and coping in the long run than the crisis event itself. You may not be able to control every aspect of your life anymore, but you can control some small part. Actually, you may have far more opportunities for control than you realize. As we go along, we'll point out these opportunities, and you'll learn to exert control in specific areas and manage the rest until circumstances change.

"I will take small steps toward healing." Commit yourself to taking things one small step at a time. Put off making any sweeping, global changes, and forget about trying to rebuild Rome in a single day. Just do what you can as you go along, and give yourself time to respond to healing.

"This too shall pass." This phrase, with its biblical ring, was the advice Charles and Kathy tried most to remember in raising their four children. Their first child, a baby boy, had been born despite complications that required Kathy to spend many long months in bed prior to delivery. When it was all over and the healthy infant was brought home, one of the senior instructors at Charles's school took him aside and passed on a bit of grandmotherly advice.

"Remember, Charles," she said, "when things get rough over the years, as they certainly will, keep in mind even during the most trying, frustrating, and desperate circumstances that *change* is the order of the universe — even the small universe of your own home. 'This too shall pass,' helped me through more than one tribulation in raising my own family."

Your crisis, too, will pass. Just when you think you can't take it anymore, remember that it's bound to change soon. A new stability will emerge from the chaos. The crisis, with all its pain and heartache and turmoil, will not last forever.

"Since I have no idea what my new life will be like, it could well be better than I ever imagined." The founder of gestalt therapy, Fritz Perls, reminds us that anxiety is actually "stage fright." It is worry about things that have not happened yet. No one has any idea what the future will be, so it makes absolutely no

sense to conjure up the worst picture you can imagine and then worry about how bad it's going to be.

When tempted to worry about what's going to happen, step back and remind yourself that things could just as easily get better; in all probability there could be a positive turn of events in your future.

"I will live in the present." The present is all we ever have to live in — the past is gone and the future is not yet here. Postpone as many major life decisions as you can. Give yourself a chance to make good use of the ideas presented in this book. Use your present to make the future better.

◆ ◆ ◆

What will happen if you practice these things? You will discover that you are keeping your options open, that you are mobilizing your strength, that resources are opening up to you that you didn't know you had. Most people have strength buried within them, lying dormant, never used. You may fear that you can't make it through this time, but you really don't know for certain because you have never been tested this hard before.

It is the nature of a crisis to shake up your stable world, to force you to reach deep within yourself for reservoirs of hidden strength, to bring out courage and hope and love in far greater measure than you ever knew existed. You may not feel courageous or hopeful or strong right now, but that does not mean your courage, hope, or strength is not there, waiting to be tapped. Keep the possibility open; you could be in for a great surprise.

WHEN YOU DON'T KNOW WHERE TO START

Your aim for the next several days or weeks is to concentrate on simply coping the best way you can, keeping as many of your options open as possible. You cannot solve all the problems you are worried about right now — that is going to take time. Begin with the idea that some things need to be done now, while others can wait. To find out which is which . . .

Make a List

Write down all the things you are thinking about right now. Nothing fancy here, simply write down all your concerns, worries, frustrations, and make a list.

Ron, for example, had just gone into business with his father. Their company was still getting organized when his father died quite unexpectedly of a heart attack. Ron's list looks like this:

How will Mom take all this; will she get sick, too?
Who's going to tell the family?
How can we afford the funeral?
Where's Dad's life insurance policy?
Why am I so upset? — I've got to take this like a man.
How can I manage the business by myself?
Will the creditors trust me to continue?
My stomach hurts — am I getting an ulcer?
Dad did it to himself; I told him to slow down!

Jack, a steelworker, showed up at the mill one day only to discover that he had been laid off. Jack's list looks like this:

How can I face Sue?
How will we ever pay the bills?
Will we be able to keep our house?
Should I sell the car?
School starts in a month. What are the kids going to do
    for clothes?
There goes the vacation I had planned on so much.
At my age, I may never find another really good job.

How do I apply for unemployment benefits?

Will my union pension be lost?

What will everyone think of me now? I know Sue's family
will think less of me — they already think I'm not as
smart or capable as her brother and Dad.

Notice the range of issues people think about; notice, too,
that some of the items are immediate concerns and others are
long range. Therefore, you will need to . . .

Identify Your Top Priorities

Go through the list you have just made and decide what has
to be done now and what can wait. Put a check mark by any
item that must be dealt with in the next few hours or days.

One way to isolate these issues is to *look for anything that, if
left unattended for the next several hours or days, could reduce your
options for the future.*

This is the cornerstone of crisis management: scanning possible actions and choosing those which both cut losses and
keep as many options open as possible.

For example, the Morris family returned home to find their
house had burned down while they were away for the weekend. Their top priority was both finding a place to spend the
next few nights and getting help for the three small children.
It was *not* immediately important whether to buy again, or
rent, or build a new house. Therefore, phone calls to their
insurance agent and their priest (who helped contact nearby
relatives) were the most important first steps.

In any crisis situation, determining your priorities — deciding what can be done later and what has to be done right away
— will help keep you from getting sidetracked, confused, and
frustrated as you try to sort through all the issues confronting
you.

Don't be at all surprised if your initial reaction is to try to handle everything at once. As you assess the situation, you will be worried about a great many things and will feel that you have to deal with all of them now.

Have another look, though. As you have seen in going through your list, some things — perhaps a great many things — can be postponed until later: weeks or months, maybe even a year or more.

Putting things off like this may seem like bad advice. It certainly runs counter to modern folk wisdom: move ahead, make time, get it done yesterday. But postponing as many decisions as you can is one of the wisest moves you can make. You are buying time for yourself, time that you can use to pull yourself together and to take care of the issues that must be dealt with right away.

Also, by postponing all but the most immediate issues, you avoid making any binding, long-term decisions in the heat of the crisis — decisions you might come to regret later on when you have had time to think.

This postponing action is not the same as ignoring the problem, ducking responsibility, or running from reality. In fact, by postponing issues you are actually managing them in a most effective way, by saying, "I will deal with this later when I can devote the proper time and energy to it."

Once you have identified what has to be done now, you are ready to . . .

Plan Your Best Move

A famous chess player once observed that, even though the grand masters can think twenty or more moves ahead, they still must play the game one move at a time. In the early stages of a crisis, don't pressure yourself to win the whole match in one move. Rather, after thinking ahead several moves, make the one move that keeps your options open and puts you on the path out of the crisis. If you are unsure of what your best next move should be, then get outside help to think it through. (See Appendix C, on how to find competent outside help.)

The moves you make, remember, are *small, concrete steps, not global changes*. A woman who has been told she has a lump in her breast, for example, might feel like scheduling immediate surgery at the best cancer hospital in the country. But her best first moves might be to:

— call her physician to see about further tests,

— ask a friend to watch her children after school for the next few days,

— call a hot line or a counselor for help in sorting through her options.

And Remember . . .

A crisis is no time to neglect your friends. *Use your social resources*. Even if family and loved ones are far away, and even if you might have to spend a few dollars on a long-distance phone call, your closest friends should be considered as people you can turn to now to help you make some of the pressing decisions you are dealing with.

You might be carrying around the myth of "I've got to conquer this alone." Many people do. You might be reluctant to call on friends during a crisis, thinking that calling on others will somehow make you dependent on them or that involving others in your troubles is a sign of weakness.

The truth is that to call on friends right now is not to become dependent upon them for life. On the contrary, it is one of the smartest moves you can make: using the resources you have available to help you get through this time of intense upheaval.

Since crises usually involve such huge problems, normal problem-solving techniques are simply overwhelmed. Your usual decision-making methods are unable to handle the situation because you are thinking about too much of the problem at once. Break it down into small chunks, and, by all means, use whatever outside resources are available — friends, clergy, family, physician.

By following the guidelines presented in this chapter you can start yourself on a course toward healing and growth. Once you have given yourself psychological first aid, allow it time to work. It will, and soon you will come to a place where you feel that you can cope once more. Then you are ready to begin thinking about your life in the weeks and months ahead — you are ready to begin drawing your own blueprint for growth.

· FOUR ·

A Blueprint for Growth

EVERY YEAR millions of Americans flee the cities for vacations in our nation's beautiful national parks. Inevitably, some of these people, so fervent in their desire to experience the wilderness, become lost. And sometimes what began as a happy family outing in the great outdoors ends in tragedy.

Of course, getting lost in the wilderness is not always fatal. Most people survive the ordeal, suffering little more than sore feet and a couple of missed meals. Park rangers and other wilderness experts remind us that the ones who survive follow a few basic rules of survival in the wilderness. Sometimes they follow them without even knowing that is what they are doing.

The same is true with psychological crises. Many people survive and grow through crises, and others do not. A study of survivors of life crises indicates that there is a natural evolution of events leading to growth. If you listen carefully when talking to survivors, you'll notice that they all talk about following the same basic principles. Whether the road to recovery was smooth or rocky, whether it was like a 100-yard dash or a long, slow marathon, they all came through it using the same survival techniques.

THE KEY TO SURVIVAL

We often think that those who survive rough times are those with the most resources to draw on. Obviously, if you have a fairly hefty savings account and lose your job, you may be able to survive the crisis of unemployment far more easily than someone who has no money in savings.

Similarly, you might have surrounded yourself with dozens of very close friends through the years. If you were suddenly to become ill, having friends around to support you, help with the household chores, run errands, and visit you would dramatically aid recovery. Your resolution of this crisis might be far different than if you lived in a strange town where you didn't know anyone and had to nurse yourself back to health alone.

An individual may be rich in friends or money, but it is not the friends or the money alone that help a person weather a crisis. These resources are helpful only because they make survival easier.

In other words, surviving a crisis does *not* depend on a big bank account, scores of friends, or exceptional skills. These things make the work easier, but survival still depends on the choices you make and what you do along the way.

For years psychologists have been studying the differences between people who grow through life crises, and those who do not. The big difference between these two groups is that the survivors — often without their own awareness — successfully take care of themselves in four important areas.

Although they may think of themselves as merely plodding along, getting by, or simply coping, we have discovered that is not the case at all. Interviews with survivors show us that there really are distinct similarities among these people — similarities missing from people who emerge as embittered, hurting human beings, closed to the future.

The survivors are those who have taken care of their bodies

along the way, found ways to express and manage intense and often painful feelings, have triumphed over the crisis mentally, and then have made concrete changes in their behavior that allow them to live in a new and changed world.

The hopeful part is that the experience of survivors can serve as a guide for the rest of us in coping with our own crises. We can follow in their footsteps.

Start right now picturing a path toward growth that passes through the four major areas of your life: physical, emotional, mental, and behavioral. Such a path exists, and others have found it and used it to carry them away from pain and hurt into wholeness and growth. This, of course, is the phoenix factor — but it doesn't snap into operation automatically. You have to apply it consciously.

Taking the path toward growth means paying attention to each of the four major areas of life. It means:

- **Taking care of your body**
- **Managing painful feelings**
- **Changing your mind**
- **Adjusting your behavior**

The following chapters of this book are devoted to showing you how you can use the phoenix factor to grow through your own crisis by working at survival in each of these areas. This is the *know-how* that is all important in crisis resolution.

Now, let's have a closer look at each of these important areas.

Taking Care of Your Body

Obviously, physical survival of the crisis experience is the most important area at the start. Unless you maintain bodily health and well-being and take steps to insure that life will continue, nothing else really matters.

As we discussed in the last chapter, in some crises death

through homicide or suicide is a real and present danger. But there are other physical dangers that accompany crises, besides dangers of violence or death. The psychological strain of the crisis always brings with it accompanying physical strain.

Muscles tighten up, leading to stomachache, stiff neck, sore back; the circulation of blood decreases, causing headaches and disturbed sleep; nerves seem raw, inviting the abuse of drugs or alcohol to soothe them.

While each of these is bad enough in itself, there is also the danger that they will lead to negative habits that could continue long after the crisis is over.

It is not uncommon for someone who quit smoking years ago suddenly to pick up the habit again following a severe marital crisis, or a setback at work. Another individual may develop a habit of nervous eating after an illness or the death of a family member.

The way you feel in the early stages of a crisis will differ from the way you feel later on. In the early stages you simply want to keep life and limb together; later, however, when your life starts to even out a bit, you will have the opportunity to do more in the areas of nutrition, exercise, and rest.

The next chapter will examine ways to take care of your body during a crisis and to improve your health in the long run. As some of our examples will show, major life crises often mark the beginning of new and more healthful lifestyles for many people.

Managing Painful Feelings

If there is any one aspect of a crisis that stands out, or one part that lingers long in remembrance, it is probably that the whole experience *feels* terrible.

During a crisis emotions are savagely thrown into turmoil. Extremes become the norm. Indeed, what make the crisis so completely devastating for many people is that the magnitude of what they are feeling is greater than anything they have ever felt before: grief, remorse, rage, anxiety, depression, guilt — all in megadoses that shock and overpower the delicate system.

If not expressed, these powerful emotions must be bottled up in some way — an act that takes tremendous amounts of energy — energy that cannot be used for other purposes, like working, playing, and loving.

Keeping powerful emotions bottled up is always a chancy endeavor. The pressure builds and cannot be released. This warps the container and usually leads to a dangerous explosion when the pressure grows too great.

People who survive a crisis, especially those who make best use of the power to grow through the crisis experience, eventually come to terms with such powerful feelings as anger, guilt, sadness, or remorse, so that these feelings don't linger on, poisoning life.

In the early stages of crisis these intense feelings need to be identified, and then allowed some form of expression. It's almost like letting some of the steam out of a pressure cooker — the release relieves some of the intensity so that you can begin making sense of your feelings, understanding what they mean in your life.

Survivors do not ignore their feelings during a crisis. Instead, they manage them, finding ways to express and understand them. Chapter Six will offer a whole range of strategies you can use to begin managing the feelings that threaten to overwhelm you and actually turn them to your advantage.

Changing Your Mind

Whether you survive and grow through a crisis depends to a large extent on how you *interpret* the experience, how you think about it.

When we listen to comments of people in crisis, we hear phrases like "I never dreamed it would happen to me!" or "I always thought my life would be different." These are repeated time and again, hinting at the enormous struggle to gain a mental grasp of the situation.

A close look at any crisis reveals that it is not the experience itself that does us in, but what it means to us, or how we think about the event. People who don't survive are those who never get past particular negative thoughts, images, beliefs, or ideas about what has happened to them.

Surviving a crisis and turning it toward growth means adapting to it mentally, adjusting your thoughts, developing new beliefs and understandings of life so that growth becomes possible.

Psychologists call this cognitive mastery, a process involving three phases. The first phase consists of getting the facts of the situation, that is, finding out what happened to cause the crisis. You do this by asking, "Why did my spouse leave me?" Or "What were the circumstances of the accident?"

It may be painful to delve into the facts of the crisis; however, just like lancing a boil or pulling an impacted tooth is a necessary, though painful, first step that leads to healing, facing the facts of a crisis is the first step toward mastering the crisis mentally.

The second phase of the cognitive-mastery process is understanding exactly how the event violates your expectations about life, learning precisely how and why it shatters dreams, or blocks goals. It may be that the event threatens your view of the world in some important way. In any case, the people who grow through a crisis learn which hopes and dreams, which expectations, or which views of the world were violated by the crisis event. In other words, they identify where the repair work is needed.

Finally, the most important phase of cognitive mastery or changing your mind is developing new images, goals, hopes, dreams, and thoughts which allow you to live in a radically changed world — the world after the crisis. Some people refer to this as a spiritual transformation, grounded in a new sense of proportion about life. Priorities change. New values are adopted. Whatever particular form this takes, changing your mind leads to a new view of how to live in the future, one that mobilizes your energy to move forward. Those people who fail to grow through the crisis never develop such a view for satisfying and productive living in the future. For these people the loss of a limb, of a relationship, of a job, of a loved one, or of a cherished hope stands forever as a roadblock to the future.

Actually, this is the same for everyone at first. The survivors, however, eventually move past the roadblock and follow a new mental map into the future. This new map is made up of revised goals or dreams, beliefs that have been informed or amended by the crisis event, and a view of life that accepts and does not deny the reality of the crisis event.

Although it often appears impossible, the new mental map — which often grows from an idea that unlocks a closed door, or a spiritual awareness or thought that suddenly takes on special healing power — is what guides survivors through the process of adjusting behavior and living in the new world.

Adjusting Your Behavior

The utter disorganization of a crisis makes "business as usual" impossible in many, if not all respects. And while you may have taken steps to survive the crisis event physically, and found ways to manage your feelings, and have come to an understanding of what has happened and how it affects the future, the process is not complete until you adjust your behavior to fit with the new circumstances of your life.

A woman who has just lost her husband, for example, may discover that a whole range of new behavioral skills are necessary for survival: she must learn how to take care of her own finances, how to attend social functions as a single person, maybe even how to fix things around the house and keep the car running smoothly.

In a crisis the basic arenas of human activity are affected: work, leisure, family and social life, and friendships. You are left with the feeling that *"nothing* will ever be the same again" — which means that you will be making adjustments in how you work, spend your leisure time, relate to your family, and so on.

These behavioral changes — learning new skills or new ways of relating to others — can lead beyond simple survival to amazing growth in new, or dormant, areas of life. This re-tooling for the work of living can bring startling new opportunities. For here, more than in any other area, the capacity for growth is at its greatest.

HEALING OLD WOUNDS — AND NEW

The four areas of life we have just briefly described apply to past crises as well as present ones. If you are going through a crisis right now, the information in the following chapters will serve as a blueprint for surviving and growing through the experience. Or, as you read along, you may find that you are still haunted by a past crisis and have never expressed your feelings about it properly, or that you have never come to understand it and interpret it so that you can move past the crisis and into the future.

If this is your situation, this may be your chance to complete the resolution process — this time toward a new and better end, even if the crisis event is years past.

There is nothing mystical or mysterious about working through a crisis, though most people are in the dark about what actually takes place. This book will demystify the growth process, explaining how to make progress in each of the four areas we've just discussed.

We have used the phoenix as a symbol of survival and growth through crisis, but another way to picture this growth process might be in terms of a baseball game. Of course, in order to score a run in baseball the batter must hit the ball and run around all four bases, touching each in turn before reaching home base.

In our game there are four bases to touch, too, as you can see in the drawing on page 43. But in our brand of baseball, you don't have to run the bases in order — touch whichever one you want, in whatever order makes sense to you. You can even run back and forth from one base to the next — tag second and go to third, run to first and back to second and then to home and over to third again. You can pitch for an inning, or sit out in the dugout for a while. It doesn't matter *how* you do it — there are no umpires to call you out.

The only rule is that in order to score you must at some time during the game make sure to touch *each* of the four bases.

If baseball isn't your game, perhaps you can think of life as an intricate tapestry made up of different patterns and figures — each based on your experiences in life and each important to the overall design. Ultimately, you want the the crisis experience to take its place alongside the other patterns in the tapestry. It should not take up more room for itself than is necessary. You don't want to embroider the experience garishly, nor do you want to ignore it — any more than you would want to tear a hole in your beautiful tapestry or leave a large expanse of blank, unfinished material.

You want the crisis to become interwoven in its place among all the other patterns and figures in your tapestry so that it is a part of the grand design of your life.

Our goal is to lead you to the place where you can say: "Yes, that happened to me. I suffered a great deal. I went through tremendous emotional pain, and felt very upset, and even thought at times that I could not go on. But I talked about it, expressed my feelings, asked for and accepted the help of friends, and found that with this, and the passage of time, the event no longer has the same hold on me that it did in the

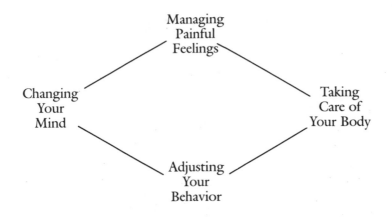

Baseball Diagram

beginning. I have even discovered that some parts of my life that were previously dormant have been strengthened in positive ways. My outlook on life is changing; I'm beginning to appreciate all that I still have and the new strengths I've found.

"And now? The emotional scars are healing, though they're still there. Yes, I can remember; I know what I went through. But the crisis is becoming just one of the many experiences that make up my total life. It is taking its place alongside other experiences, so that I am ready to go on now. And though at times I relive some of the pain, the hard work is over. I've grown, and I'm ready to face the future."

· FIVE ·

Taking Care of Your Body

WHEN YOU'RE IN A CRISIS, the last thing you want is to hear someone telling you to "eat right and get plenty of exercise," to "find some way to relax and let loose of all that tension." You are hurting; your world is in upheaval, your life turned upside-down.

You can't eat. There is no time to exercise — you're too busy driving back and forth to the hospital, or trying to find a job, or just trying to get through the day. Rest and relaxation sound nice, but you are so keenly aware of the emotional pain throbbing in you that rest in inconceivable, and relaxation impossible.

It's true — the very nature of a crisis is directly opposed to good physical health. But something else is true, too: You have to take care of your body first; otherwise nothing else you do will matter.

Obviously, if your health totally deteriorates, or if you die as a result of this crisis, it won't make much difference how you manage the rest of it. If you don't take steps to protect yourself from injury, from taking too many pills or drinking too much alcohol, or from deliberately taking your own life, then you will never have the chance to understand the crisis, to make adjustments in your life, to grow into your future.

The basic requirement then is to take the necessary steps toward keeping your body in good working order — as good as you possibly can under the circumstances — during the toughest part of the crisis. And although it might seem strange to think of it now, you can also be on the lookout for hidden opportunities to improve your physical well-being as a result of the crisis.

Improve your physical health? This is a hell of a time to start on a health kick, right? Anyway, how could anyone possibly get serious about health during something so bad as getting a divorce, being fired, or finding out you must have surgery for a heart condition?

Dan was a heavy smoker and something of a workaholic. Added to that, Dan's wife, Irene, had severe emotional problems — she had been in and out of state hospitals for years. Dan had always borne the burden of caring for her, never once thinking about what the stress was doing to him.

The crisis came when, without warning, Dan suffered a heart attack and underwent open-heart surgery. During his recovery, Dan struggled to pull his life back together. One day his physician told him that above all else he had to quit smoking, and now was as good a time as any. At first, Dan thought his doctor was joking; there was no way on God's green earth that he could even go a single day without a cigarette.

Still, when he went home from the hospital he was determined to do his best to quit smoking. He quickly decided that he had to have something to do when the urge to light up a cigarette came over him. That something was exercise, which was also good for his heart. He changed his daily routine so that every day at noon he forced himself to leave his office and go for a walk. His walks became longer, and he started jogging a little, too.

Dan discovered that jogging was a much-needed break —

it helped him manage the stress that built up during the day. He also found that he could not smoke and continue jogging, and since running gave him so much more satisfaction, he did not light up again.

His crowning achievement came when he entered a 10,000-meter race sponsored by a local running club. Crossing the finish line marked, for Dan, six years of nonsmoking and increased health. He felt better than ever physically and was enjoying a radically changed lifestyle that had begun at his breaking point, on the surgeon's table.

TWO OBJECTIVES

The two objectives to work on in taking care of your body during a crisis are first, to protect yourself from bodily harm and second, to look for opportunities to improve your health in the long run. In meeting these two objectives it is not uncommon for a person to come through a crisis in better physical health than if the crisis had never happened.

Remember that one very hopeful aspect of any crisis is that where danger exists, opportunity also exists. Many times, a crisis will force us to give up patterns of living that are actually doing us great harm. Sometimes old ways have to break down completely before we understand that there are better ways of taking care of ourselves.

The ideas presented in this chapter are intended to help you meet the two objectives — to help you protect yourself from bodily harm and to open the door to better ways of taking care of yourself in the future.

This time of crisis just might be the time for you to begin learning better and more enjoyable ways of eating, exercising, and relaxing.

WHAT HAPPENS TO YOUR BODY DURING A CRISIS?

The mind and body are inextricably linked together. Decades of psychological research indicate that a change in one can produce a change in the other with a ripple effect on your emotions, relationships, and behavior. So, it makes sense that during an emotional crisis your body will hurt in one way or another.

Think of the last time you experienced a crisis, or when the crisis you're going through now first struck. Something happened, you saw something, or heard a message from someone, and before you were even aware of it your stomach may have tightened into a ball, or you may have "lost your breath" for a moment, or felt dizzy and sick.

Our bodies react to news we hear; they react to the way we receive news — in particular, they react to how we *think* about what we receive. Crisis events, so powerful and potentially destructive, dictate significant changes in our individual life patterns. Adjusting to these changes can cause stress, which can lead to physical illness.

In the early 1950s, for example, Thomas Holmes, a University of Washington psychiatrist, discovered that among tuberculosis patients the onset of the disease usually followed a series of very disruptive events: death of a loved one, demands of a new job, marriage, moving to a new home. The stress of these changes did not cause the disease — it still took tuberculosis bacteria for that — but tension and stress actively promoted the disease process. He learned that merely discussing upsetting events could produce physical symptoms in a patient.

The impact of stressful life events on physical health has been proven many times. Medical doctors now recognize that emotional stress can cause severe physical deterioration. An experience of intense anxiety, anger, fear, or depression throws your physical processes out of balance, and body cells actually start deteriorating. If this downward trend is not reversed immediately you may become more susceptible to a whole host of diseases — colds, heart ailments, flu, even cancer.

Perhaps the most significant new discovery about stress is its harmful effect on the body's immune system. Researchers have discovered that the body's production of disease- and cancer-fighting cells is suppressed by chronic stress.

Worry, anger, anxiety, depression, guilt, fear, resentment, and other feelings associated with crisis will over time take a physical toll on your body. You cannot prevent your body from reacting at first. But you *can* recognize that you are in a crisis situation and under a great deal of stress, that your body is in jeopardy, and that you will need to take appropriate steps to protect yourself.

FIRST THINGS FIRST

Taking care of your body is probably one of the last things you're thinking about in the heat of a crisis. So many other pressing and painful issues swallow you up. Most likely you are thinking of something else right now — a spouse or loved one who has left or become ill; the news that you have been fired or transferred or laid off; the thousand and one things that go along with a major event, such as moving to a strange city, starting a new venture, getting married, arranging for a funeral . . . and so on.

Even though you may not be thinking about taking care of your body right now, you may be aware of certain physical complaints. You may feel dragged out, flat; or perhaps uptight and ready to explode. You may find it hard to eat or sleep. You might feel weak, unable to go on another step.

At this time when your thoughts are far from your physical health, we want to remind you of two important checkpoints:

1. Do whatever you can to keep body and soul together.

2. Protect yourself against thoughts and actions that could endanger your life.

Let's take the second one first.

Stayin' Alive

One of the most frightening aspects of a crisis is that sometimes very destructive thoughts and impulses are unleashed. For the first time in your life you may entertain thoughts of suicide, or of lashing out at someone else. These thoughts are another indication of how high the stakes can be during a crisis.

As scary as they are, thoughts of giving up are not uncommon at the onset of crisis: "I can't go on!" or "It's no use. I might as well end it all right now!" Suicidal thoughts and impulses are a profound reflection of how bad the situation appears to you. And they should not be ignored.

The same goes for thoughts of harming other people, too. Since the primary goal of physical survival early in any crisis is to prevent bodily harm — to yourself and anyone near you — when thoughts of "ending it all" or "getting revenge" come up you must check yourself and take protective measures.

Of course, as we pointed out in Chapter Three, simply having thoughts of hurting yourself or somebody else does not mean you are dangerous. But the thought together with the opportunity to carry it out is a red flag that signals danger. In other words, where there is a will (the dangerous thought) and a way (the opportunity to carry out the thought) there could well be trouble. The most common lethal opportunities are buying a weapon, obtaining pills, drinking too much, driving while depressed or angry.

When both *thought* and *opportunity* to do physical harm are present, the danger must be taken seriously and the following steps taken:

1. Ask for help. Call a counselor, your minister, rabbi, or priest, or call a crisis hot line to talk over your problems and ask for assistance. You need help in sorting through the problem and deciding how to handle your destructive feelings.

2. Remove any weapons or other items that might allow you to carry out your destructive thoughts. Do you have a handgun? — Get rid of it. Pills? — Flush them. Alcohol? — Lock it up. Put the means of destruction as far away from you as possible so that an impulsive act will not result in long-term damage to yourself or someone else.

3. Remind yourself continually that your violent impulses *will* change. Do not act on something now that will change in a few hours or days. It will help to concentrate on the positive aspects of your situation (reasons to live) and to seek outside help to cope with the negative (reasons to die or hurt someone). Keep all your options open until you have a chance to talk things over with a counselor.

Most people who end up hurting themselves or someone else do so because they see absolutely no hope for change in the future. A crisis is, after all, a time when all the normal patterns of life are disrupted — sometimes so severely disrupted that it may seem there is no reason to go on living. But experience with survivors shows that the dark, gloomy, hopeless thoughts and feelings *do* change — sometimes surprisingly quickly.

Therefore, wait for the change. Since your thoughts and feelings will change soon, why make any decisions or take any actions now that you may regret in a few hours? Wait. Keep your options open. See what the change in thoughts and feelings will bring.

Keeping Body and Soul Together

What can you do when the stress of the crisis is so great that you lose all interest in food? Or what can you do when the crisis sends you in the opposite direction — nervously eating anything and everything in the house? Or when the press of a changed schedule makes it impossible to sit down to a calm and peaceful meal?

The answers to these questions vary, of course, depending on your situation. But one rule applies to everyone in crisis: do whatever you can to supply your body with essential nutrients.

If you are having trouble eating solid food, perhaps one of those nutritional supplements that athletes drink in liquid form would be helpful. If you are compulsively overeating, it may be that stocking up on a good supply of fresh fruit and vegetables will help — that way your nervous munching will supply vitamins and fiber instead of empty calories. If finding time to cook and eat a decent meal is the problem, calling on a friend to help you out by preparing some meals for you may be the smartest thing you could do. Whatever your situation, you will find that taking a good multiple vitamin tablet will help replenish the nutrients burned up by stress.

During a routine examination, a doctor spotted a shadow on David's x-ray. The small tumor was found to be malignant and surgery was planned immediately. Suddenly Jane's life was in chaos; not only did she have to cope with the fear of losing her husband, she also had to deal with the immediate difficulty of running their home and managing life for her two small children while her husband was in the hospital.

For weeks her life was little more than getting up early in the morning and throwing some sort of breakfast together for herself and the kids, getting everyone dressed and dropping off the children at school, going to work and then rushing to spend her lunch hour at the hospital, dashing back to work to finish out the day and then leaving in time to pick up the kids as school let out, driving home for a quick supper before running back to the hospital that evening.

Jane's life became so hectic, and the demands of her schedule so great, that eating and sleeping became difficult: she tossed and turned all night, hardly able to close her eyes; and she had a hard time swallowing the few bites of food that she managed to grab for herself. She noticed that she was feeling more and more physical tension in her muscles; she felt strung out most of the day. The grueling pace was wearing her to a frazzle.

Jane found that, like most people in crisis, she was exhausting herself in the effort to meet everyone else's needs but was neglecting her own. Her own eating habits were deteriorating: a half-piece of toast in the morning, gulped down with coffee, a candy bar for lunch, dinner of fast-food hamburgers and cokes. She had also begun drinking a couple of glasses of wine at night to help her go to sleep, although the effect was minimal and she woke up an hour or two later.

It was David's doctor who finally called a halt to all this. He noticed that she looked exhausted, and told her that she would have to start looking out for herself if she was to survive David's illness. Jane realized he was right and, though it was far from easy, she started making small changes in the way she was getting through the day.

Eating right was difficult for Jane because she was so pressed for time. Finally, in frustration she admitted to a friend that she hated planning meals and cooking while David was in the hospital waiting to see her. To her surprise, the friend offered to do the grocery shopping, prepare some meals ahead of time, and put them in the freezer for Jane to pull out and heat up. Her friend also stocked up Jane's refrigerator with plenty of fresh fruit, juice, and vegetables that she washed and cut up so they could be pulled out and tossed into lunches or eaten as snacks anytime. The improvement in how Jane felt —switching to fruit instead of candy bars, and juice instead of coffee and cola — gave her extra energy to begin coping again.

She discovered that the key to remaining on top of the situation was to take care of her own body. She got a neighbor to watch the kids so that she could get out for a vigorous walk every other day. Sometimes she and her son rode their bikes in the evening after dinner, which also gave them some needed time together. Later, this weekly exercise routine fit in perfectly with her husband's recovery.

When David returned home the whole family began taking short walks together, and the practice led over time to a regular exercise habit that they built into their lives and continue to this day.

As we all know, the changes demanded by a crisis can be quite radical. But the fact is many of these changes can be good. Notice too that you don't have to make sweeping, revolutionary changes all at once. Start by making small adjustments to allow your body to get at least minimal nutrition and exercise. Don't feel guilty if you cannot do as well for yourself as you would like right now. A crisis is a bad time to go on a diet, for example, or begin a strenuous aerobics regime.

Simply do what you can, making whatever changes you can to keep body and soul together. Look for those areas where small adjustments can improve nutrition, relaxation, and exercise patterns. The rest of this chapter offers hints on getting started, but first a few words about . . .

AVOIDING FALSE STARTS AND TRAPS

We live in a culture where it is popular to anesthetize any and all pain. We do it in a number of ways, alcohol and pills being the most common. Alcohol brings a sense of numbness and false security to mind and body. A wide variety of over-the-counter medications, some for calming and others for stimulating, are readily available.

But the use of alcohol and pills during a crisis can become a dangerous and sometimes deadly trap. Protective measures need to be taken from the beginning to make sure you don't fall into this trap. The rules here are straightforward:

- Don't take medications without the supervision of your physician.
- Don't use alcohol and pills together; some combinations can be deadly.
- Medications are only for *temporary* coping. Prolonged use can lead to dependency or addiction.

Remember that some of the emotional pain you are experiencing can be used to your advantage; it is actually helpful to know when and how you hurt, what sets off the bad spells. If you continually anesthetize the pain away, you are actually interfering with your natural resolution process and halting your own recovery and growth.

A PATH TOWARD HEALTH

For every human being there is a natural rhythm of *exercise* and *rest*. For optimal functioning this rhythm is maintained with proper *nutrition*.

As we have seen, in a crisis the normal balance is easily upset — we may lose ourselves in work; sleep eludes us; we forget to exercise; we eat poorly, skip meals, or eat too much; we may drink too much. Therefore, taking the path toward health means *taking steps that result in proper exercise, nutrition, and rest*.

The emphasis here is on the word *steps*. After the initial days and weeks of shock and numbness, start taking those first small steps to move along on the path toward health by achieving a natural rhythm or balance of nutrition, exercise, and rest.

There are tremendous opportunities for growth here! In time of crisis, when you begin making a determined effort to eat, rest, and exercise properly, you can latch on to new health habits that can make your future far better than your past — before the crisis. You can start a regular exercise program, make a conscious decision to eat more nutritious meals, establish a regular work/sleep rhythm.

Grandma Rose, aged eighty-four, when explaining her longevity, alert mind, and zest for life, talks about the time she was "hit by a freight train" — that's how she describes the terrible turmoil her life was thrown into when her husband died.

Up to that time she had been a traditional mother: caring for her five children, running a clean, orderly home, denying herself in many ways so that her husband and children would have a "little extra" of the family's limited resources. Becoming a widow at age fifty-three forced her to develop some of her special hidden talents.

While she had always made a point of preparing nutritious meals and making sure her family got a good night's sleep, she realized now just how important these things were, not only for her children, but for herself as well. Her own health was vital — she was the only parent her kids had, therefore she had to take care of herself. In the morning after breakfast, when the kids were off to school, Rose began taking long walks to help her sort out all the various things she needed to think about and plan for. She noticed that she felt better after these walks and went about the rest of her day with much more vigor: her walks led to her becoming interested in fitness.

She enrolled in a fitness course at a local college, and this led to a full-time college career that culminated in a master's degree in health education. Upon graduation, Rose took a job as a health instructor in the public school system and began a rewarding second career.

Looking back, there was obviously much sadness over the loss of her husband, but Rose attributes her success and happiness over the next thirty years to the changes she was forced to make during the original crisis. "I knew I had to take care of myself, and I did," she explains. "Discovering that was one of the best things that ever happened to me."

As you think about your own situation, remember that each person has different needs in the three main health areas — nutrition, exercise, rest — which means we can't present one program to benefit everyone. Still, there are general principles of nutrition, exercise, and rest that apply to all of us.

Nutrition

The chief difficulty of a crisis from a nutritional point of view is that eating habits (good or bad) are thrown off. You lose all taste for food and can't eat, you overeat, or you consume the wrong things (stimulants, like coffee or colas, or depressants, like alcohol).

Poor nutrition leaves you feeling weak or lethargic, with no energy, or so "wired and hyper" you can't think straight. Whatever the case, you are in no condition to proceed effectively in dealing with your crisis.

Also, since the stress associated with the crisis takes its own physical toll, you will have a greater need for certain nutrients than when you are in more normal circumstances. Stress on the body combined with poor eating habits leads to even greater nutritional deficiencies.

The best way to combat this downward nutritional spiral is to force yourself into a positive routine and to police bad habits such as abuse of alcohol or medications. Therefore:

• Eat regular meals. If you are tempted to skip meals, eat smaller portions more frequently during the day.

• Forget junk, snack, and convenience foods.

• Include an abundance of natural and high-fiber foods: whole grains, vegetables, and fruits.

• Take a vitamin tablet or other nutritional supplement to help counter vitamin and mineral depletion due to stress.

• If you are tempted to overeat, stock up on natural foods — fresh fruit, juice, raw vegetables of all kinds — foods that will allow you to eat your fill while giving you the nutrients you need.

• Avoid drinking too much alcohol. (Especially avoid driving after you have been drinking so that you will not endanger your own life or someone else's, thus compounding the crisis.)

• Monitor your caffeine intake. Coffee, tea, and colas can make you more uptight. If you are having trouble sleeping, remember that cheese and milk products are rich in the amino acid tryptophan, a natural sleep-promoting substance. Dairy products can be helpful in inducing sleep at bedtime and also produce a calming effect during the day.

Physical Exercise

Vigorous exercise is one of the best ways to reduce tension and stress during a crisis. Exercise is part of the body's natural rhythm, but if you are not already working out it will not help you to throw yourself into a strenuous exercise program. The dangers will likely outweigh the benefits. You may pull muscles, injure yourself, or build up such an aversion to exercise that you will never want to try it again under more normal circumstances.

Still, there is no better way to reduce tension, free your mind for a while, and prepare your body for sleep at night. As you start, remember the following:

• Consult your doctor before beginning any new exercise program.

• Remember the three phases of complete exercise — proper warm-up with stretching, slowly raising the rate of heartbeat 75 to 85 percent of your peak rate for 30 minutes, followed by a proper cooling-down period. (You can determine your proper exercise range by subtracting your age from 220. For example, if you are forty years old, your maximum heart rate is 180 beats per minute. Your exercise should work to raise your pulse rate to between 135 and 153 beats per minute — which is 75 to 85 percent of your maximum heart rate of 180.)

• Good exercise is one of the best tools for appropriately channeling the physical effects of stress, and may also stimulate the body's natural disease defenses.

• Good exercise can produce significant psychological and emotional benefits: more flexibility in thinking, increased sense of self-sufficiency, strengthened self-concept, improved self-acceptance, less tendency to blame others, less depression.

• An exercise program of at least half an hour three times a week is important at any time of life, but can be especially helpful during a crisis. It reduces the negative effects of stress and starts you on a path toward growth.

Rest

The other end of the body's natural rhythm is rest. This is what most people find hardest to achieve during a crisis. The tremendous emotional and mental anguish associated with a crisis event seems designed to wipe out any opportunity for natural rest and relaxation.

It is common for sleep and rest to be interrupted during the initial stages of a crisis. And this is in itself no great danger, as long as it does not eventually lead to long-term sleep problems. The initial lack of sleep is not your biggest problem — it is your *worry* about your inability to sleep you have to watch out for.

You lie awake all night worrying, "How in the world can I work tomorrow when I can't get to sleep tonight? I'll be dead on my feet!" Thinking this way compounds the problem by increasing anxiety, which in turn makes it harder to get to sleep.

As with other health problems, many chronic sleep disorders can be directly traced to life crises: a marital problem, difficulties at work, financial worries, severe illness, and so on.

Dr. David Buchholz, chief resident in neurology at Johns Hopkins Hospital, tells us that in times of crisis people struggle to fall asleep for several nights, and then continue to struggle long after the situation is under control. This is because a cycle has developed whereby the act of struggling to fall asleep becomes an anxiety-provoking event; the anxiety then continues to interfere with normal sleep patterns.

Dr. Buchholz offers these ideas for help in sleeping:

• Establish a regular sleep schedule and adhere to it.

• Avoid heavy meals, excessive alcohol, caffeine, or strenuous exercise right before bedtime.

• Avoid sedatives or tranquilizers. These medications are useful only in the short term. Continued use may cause chronic insomnia because the drugs are habit-forming, quickly lose their effectiveness, and cause the quality of sleep to deteriorate.

• Set aside a comfortable place to sleep that is not being used by someone else for watching TV, playing the stereo, or reading.

• Have a snack of milk or cheese before bed.

• Avoid napping during the day to "make up" for sleep lost at night. Napping insures you won't be sleepy at your regular bedtime.

• Do not let yourself lie sleepless in bed for longer than thirty minutes. If you are having trouble falling asleep it is best to get out of bed and engage in some restful activity, like reading or listening to soothing music, until drowsiness overtakes you. (This inhibits the destructive anxiety cycle over the inability to sleep.)

• Some troubles can be "put to bed" for the night by writing them down on a piece of paper. Once written down, you can forget about them until you're ready to deal with them the next day.

• Remember that the lack of sleep will not hurt you nearly

so much as *worrying* about not sleeping. You can expect to get less sleep during the early phases of a crisis.

COMBATING STRESS WITH RELAXATION

Since tense muscles and tense emotions virtually go hand in hand, the best way to combat stress is through relaxation; it is just not possible to feel stress while completely relaxed. Interestingly enough, relaxing physically not only reduces physical stress, it also effectively reduces mental stress as well. It is almost as if the relaxed body will not allow the brain to produce those tension-making anxious or fearful thoughts. During a crisis, however, relaxation may be very difficult to achieve.

One of the most reliable and effective ways to deal with physical and emotional stress is called "progressive relaxation." Developed by Edmund Jacobson in 1938, the technique involves nothing more than simply tensing and untensing different muscle groups in the body. The idea is that through deliberate contraction and release, muscles can be made to "give up" their tension. Once tension is given up, the muscle naturally relaxes. Milk the tension out of all the major muscle groups in the body and you will effectively produce a state of deep relaxation that is incompatible with stress of any type.

The technique is simple and with a little practice can be mastered by anyone. It will help if you follow the guidelines below:

- Find a quiet room where you will not be disturbed or distracted. Keep the lights dim.
- Choose a comfortable bed, couch, or overstuffed recliner. All parts of your body must be supported without strain; otherwise you will not be able to relax completely.
- Wear loose-fitting clothing. Remove any tight

clothing or undergarments, as well as shoes, eye-glasses, and contact lenses.

You are now ready to begin. Start by practicing the movements described below:

1. Right and left hand/forearm — Make a very tight fist.

2. Right and left upper arm — Press your elbow down into the armrest of the chair or into the bed. While pressing down, move your upper arm toward your rib cage.

3. Forehead — Raise your eyebrows as high as you can. (If this movement does not produce tension, try making a deep frown.)

4. Middle face — With your eyelids shut tightly, wrinkle your nose.

5. Jaws — While pressing your tongue to the roof of your mouth, clench your teeth tightly.

6. Neck — Pull your chin down to your chest, and at the same time pull your head back with the muscles at the rear of your neck.

7. Shoulders and upper back — Shrug your shoulders as if you were trying to touch your ears.

8. Stomach — Suck your stomach inward while at the same time forcing it downward. Make it hard, as if you were preparing to be hit in the stomach by a fist.

9. Right and left thigh — Try bending your knee with the muscles at the back of your thigh while holding it rigid with muscles on top of your thigh.

10. Right and left calf — Bend your foot upward toward your shin as if you were trying to touch your shin with your toes.

When you are familiar with how each movement feels you are ready to begin using progressive relaxation to combat stress. Below are some basic instructions:

• Start by making yourself as comfortable as possible.

• Settle back until you feel comfortable and completely supported.

• Take a deep breath. Fill your lungs with air and hold your breath for seven seconds.

• Release your breath and let yourself begin to relax, letting go of the tension in your body.

• Tense the muscles of your hand and forearm. Hold that tension for five to seven seconds. Study it; be aware of what this tension feels like.

• Relax. Release the tension immediately and completely, not gradually. Feel the relaxation spread into your arm and hand. Study it; be aware of the difference between relaxation and tension. Enjoy the pleasant sensation for twenty to thirty seconds.

• Repeat the procedure: 1. Tense the muscles and hold for five to seven seconds (find a time length that feels right for you); focus on the tension. 2. Release the muscles; concentrate on the feeling of relaxation for twenty to thirty seconds. Notice the difference between the two feelings. Enjoy the pleasant sensations as your muscles loosen and relax.

• Move on to the next muscle grouping (Item 2 from the list on page 61) and perform the recommended movement. Repeat it, and then move on to the next muscle group, and the next, and so on until you have completed all the movements twice for the remaining muscle groups.

• As you lie without moving, mentally explore each of the muscle groups you have relaxed. If you feel any remaining tension in any area simply repeat the tense/relax movement for the area. If you are free of tension, just quietly enjoy your calm, peaceful feelings.

• End by imagining yourself in a calm, peaceful scene — it might be the green security of a quiet forest; or a sunlit beach, with you alone, listening to the gentle ocean waves. Imagine yourself anywhere you feel safe and secure, and at peace. Simply visualize the place in your mind and picture yourself there, completely at ease, rested and relaxed, untroubled by the events of the outside world. Enjoy this peaceful state for ten minutes, or for as long as you like.

You may find it easier to record the above instructions into a tape recorder — along with the proper timing cues. This frees you to concentrate on the movement without having to remember what do do next.

Progressive relaxation produces the most benefits when it is practiced twice a day. Once you have practiced it for a few days you will find yourself able to relax more easily and much more quickly. As with any skill, practice makes a great difference; but once it is learned, deep relaxation — whether using the technique described above, or another, such as Hatha Yoga —is a most effective weapon against stress.

TRY SOMETHING NEW

The whole idea behind this chapter has been to (1) increase energy and (2) decrease the negative effects of physical stress. You need to be healthy and alert to deal with your feelings, to think through your problems, and to make the behavioral changes necessary to grow into your future.

The suggestions given in this section on nutrition, exercise, and rest are only that — suggestions. Do not worry if you feel you cannot pull off a complete change in health habits right in the middle of a crisis. That is not the idea at all.

We realize that things may be bad for you right now. You may be having a difficult time coping. Your normal routine may have broken down completely. None of your usual methods of solving problems are working. Now might be a good time to try something new.

Find a few areas where you might make small changes and begin making them one at a time. Experiment a little and see what works for you. Try one thing today and maybe another tomorrow. Health isn't a huge mountain you have to climb all at once — you get to the top a step at a time. Over time, the steps add up to a lot of distance covered.

Try experimenting in little ways with how you eat, how you exercise, the way you relax. Try a few of the things we've mentioned and see what happens. We believe that you will find the gains can be tremendous for you — even in a very troubled time. You may come out with a whole new lifestyle.

At the very least, you can come out healthy and intact, which is the main objective of taking care of your body.

Again, the point is not to create an obstacle for you to overcome or to throw another hurdle in your path. Instead, we want to offer concrete suggestions toward physical survival — suggestions that will help counter any tendency toward chronic health problems in the future.

Try something new. It should help you feel better right now, sleep better right now, and build the energy you need to begin life anew.

SIX

Managing Painful Feelings

FOR PEOPLE living along the southern coasts of the United States a hurricane can mean disaster. The gale-force winds send towering walls of water inland to wreck all in their path — smashing houses and automobiles, breaking trees and telephone poles, throwing life into chaotic turmoil.

Soon the storm passes, and the sun comes out and the wind dies away. The rain stops. But even though the hurricane has passed, the waves continue to roll in.

People living along the coast know that the sea continues to run high long after the storm is gone. Angry waves still pound the beach — sometimes for days afterward.

This is an apt metaphor for what happens in a crisis. The event itself may strike quickly and move on. But we are left with powerful feelings and emotions that surge painfully long after the crisis has passed.

IT HURTS!

Jack and Jeanne were a young couple who had been married for only four years. They were working very hard at their different jobs, saving money to buy a house of their own. And though they seldom had money for luxuries, Jack was happy and thought Jeanne was, too.

One day Jack came home from work and Jeanne matter-offactly announced that she was sick of being married and wanted a life of her own again. She said, "Our marriage was a big mistake. I want to travel, get away from all these pressures for a while. Maybe go back to school and get my degree. I want to be with other people and date other men."

Jack knew that she was serious. He felt as if he had been punched in the stomach. Suddenly, all the air went out of him and he had to fight for breath. For a moment, he could not speak. Then, fighting back tears, he mumbled a few inarticulate questions, trying to keep himself together in the face of an overwhelming shock.

Three days later Jack moved out of their apartment because he could not stand to be around Jeanne anymore. His emotions had taken a completely different turn. Uptight, anxious, with a pain in his stomach, he walked through his daily life feeling like a ticking time bomb about to explode, all the while hoping nothing would set him off.

Alone at night in his rented room, he would cry — the first time since childhood that he had cried about anything. He felt stupid and weak crying over a woman. It seemed to him that he was losing his masculinity.

The pattern continued for the next few weeks: during the day, Jack was a ball of tension, fearful that someone would discover his damning secret; at night he cried in hopeless despair over his failed marriage and dismal future.

For many people, the powerful feelings that accompany a crisis are what make everything worse. It is bad enough to lose a loved one or a job or a relationship, or to face a new and threatening challenge — but the emotional upset stands in the way of everything you do to cope with the crisis.

You wish the negative feelings like anger, bitterness, hate, guilt, sadness, or anxiety would simply go away. But they won't.

Many self-help books and articles imply that such negative

feelings as anger, guilt, bitterness, and other very powerful emotions are not healthy and that we should live in such a way that we do not get angry, become anxious or tense, or feel fear. "Be calm, cool, mellow," they suggest. "Don't get worked up over things you can't control anyway."

The fact is, however, that this advice simply won't work in a crisis situation. The crisis event and its impact on your life are too overwhelming, too painful.

You simply cannot mellow pain away.

During a crisis you will find it impossible to get rid of painful feelings in any quick, sure-fire way. They linger on; they interfere with your life.

BURIED FEELINGS

Ed, a steel plant foreman, had worked hard for his company for eleven years and was looking forward to a big increase in pay at the beginning of his twelfth year. Instead, his plant closed and he was laid off.

At first he tried to keep his disappointment down, saying it was only temporary. Everyone who asked him about it got the same answer: "Oh, they'll start rehiring any day now."

But the plant did not reopen. Faced with the cutoff of his unemployment benefits, Ed started looking for another job, only to find that he was in competition with much younger men who could work for less money than he needed.

On the day that he received his last unemployment check, Ed did not come home. That evening, his wife was notified that Ed had wrecked his car under an overpass downtown and was badly injured. Witnesses said he was driving like a crazy man and had deliberately aimed the car at a concrete pylon.

One harmful consequence of unexpressed feelings is that instead of going away they often fester and grow, building until, much like an aerosol can thrown into a fire, they explode.

Ed was angry about being laid off, but he never expressed that anger to anyone, not even to his wife. He kept it inside him with the lid clamped down, denying what he was feeling. One day the pent-up anger exploded, and Ed drove into the concrete at sixty miles per hour.

Besides a new job, what Ed needed was a way to manage all the hurt, disappointment, and anger he felt. Even more, he needed a way to turn these feelings to his advantage — to see them for what they are: signposts pointing the way through the maze.

While most of us are experts at handling pleasant feelings — joy, happiness, affection, gratitude — we know very little about managing unpleasant ones. Negative feelings frighten us and make people around us uncomfortable, so we try to avoid them if at all possible.

Our society actually encourages us to avoid dealing with painful feelings. It says, "Take it easy. Get a grip on yourself. Be strong." This attitude is reinforced time and again in many ways. At a funeral, for example, you'll often hear comments regarding the grief-stricken family members: "Isn't she holding up well?" or "He certainly is in control."

The implication is that persons who "hold up" and are "in control" are those who do not express their feelings. Thus we are taught to keep painful emotions to ourselves, to avoid them or bury them and not let them out. Better to keep them down, control them, lest they get out of hand.

Underlying all this is the idea that emotions are irrational and should not be openly expressed because they will keep us from dealing rationally with our problems. Unfortunately for a person in crisis, simply denying, burying, or ignoring painful feelings can have long-lasting, harmful consequences.

Of course, these intense painful feelings may not always explode dramatically in the way Ed's did. They may simply simmer away deep inside, consuming more and more vital energy, sapping away strength. They can, like a cancer, gnaw at the fiber of your emotional well-being, upsetting the normal balance of physical health. Our bodies and emotions are interlocking systems. When something happens in one system, it affects the other systems, too. An emotional blow can manifest itself in a physical complaint.

Painful feelings will not just go away; they will eventually come out one way or another. They might come out as insomnia, as backaches, an ulcer, a mysterious pain, or nausea. Some people get headaches; others get skin rashes, or lose weight. Often this build-up of negative feelings will aggravate an old wound or injury, or it will masquerade as some other unexplained physical ailment, striking where the body is naturally weakest — for one a sinus condition, for another an arthritic joint. The list is endless.

HIDDEN OPPORTUNITIES

But bad as this is, it isn't the whole story. There is good news about painful feelings, too. As we shall see, feelings can be a bright beacon in the night, pointing out the way to healing and growth.

Painful feelings often provide your very first clue to how the crisis is stirring up old unfinished business from your past, and guide you toward reordering your life for the future. A Geiger counter ticks loudly when a prospector wanders into an area rich in uranium — intense feelings do much the same thing for you psychologically. They tell you that you have stumbled onto something very important from your past, or that you are entering an area critical to your future.

Learning what these painful feelings are trying to tell you is not as difficult as you may think. The key lies in dealing with them so they don't overwhelm or defeat you, but instead serve their useful purpose of pointing you toward growth.

A SECRET FROM PSYCHOTHERAPY

A cornerstone of psychotherapy is *catharsis* — an emotional letting-go of feelings, expressing them, getting them out. Sadly, most people labor under so many myths and misconceptions about painful feelings that they tend to keep themselves bottled up, fearing what might happen if they let go.

Much of the magic of a psychotherapy session is a direct result of the atmosphere of openness, in which a person can talk freely about his or her feelings of sadness or grief or depression or anger and then begin to understand what these feelings mean. This is a very basic and simple fact of growing through a crisis. Let's take a closer look.

Managing painful feelings in working through a crisis means:

— Identifying your feelings
— Expressing them
— Analyzing their meaning
— Controlling their potentially negative effects

Identify Your Feelings
Simply putting a label on what you are feeling can be half the battle. Sometimes, just knowing *what* you are dealing with can make for a real breakthrough.

Let's think again of the case of Jack, mentioned earlier in this chapter. Several weeks after separating from his wife and moving out of their apartment, Jack was talking to a counselor about his feelings.

Until seeing the counselor, Jack had been preoccupied with the *events* of the crisis: his wife's shocking announcement, their separation, facing other people at work and dodging their questions, nights of tears and frustration. He knew that his body hurt, but Jack had few words to describe what was going on inside him emotionally. He couldn't talk about it.

The therapist listened to his story and began telling Jack

what he was hearing. To his own surprise, the conversation brought some relief to Jack, which prompted him to discuss his feelings further. "I am sad," he said. "And I'm depressed about the future. I'm afraid of what my friends think of me — I'm embarrassed to be around them because I feel like such a fool. I'm also very angry at Jeanne for what she's done to me."

Somehow, Jack found himself putting words to all the things that had been bottled up inside him, churning away for weeks. The very act of naming them brought relief to him, and for the first time he recognized what he was up against. This was the first step toward managing his feelings, and taking it started him on a path toward growth.

For some people it is quite easy to identify what they are feeling. But if you are like Jack, it could be a difficult task because you may be a little out of touch with the emotional part of yourself. Perhaps your feelings have been ignored, denied, or suppressed so long that you are having difficulty knowing exactly *what* you feel right now.

This is fairly normal. A good way to start identifying your feelings is to take a look at the list of feeling words on page 72.

Which ones apply to you right now? Probably the negative ones. Or maybe you go back and forth, in a frightening way — first depressed, then giddy.

Another way to get in touch with what you're feeling during a crisis is to observe your thoughts and fantasies and to observe your own behavior. There is a distinct connection between the mental and emotional states, and between the physical and emotional states. Emotions have physical correlates as well as mental correlates. This is easy to observe.

If you're angry, your muscles may tighten, adrenalin may pump through your body as if you are preparing to attack. If you're anxious, your stomach may tense up or flutter, your throat may become dry, or your palms sweat. If you're de-

FEELINGS CHECKLIST

Abandoned	Distracted	Impulsive	Remorseful
Abused	Distrusting	Inadequate	Repressed
Accepted	Doomed	Incompetent	Repulsed
Affectionate	Doubtful	Inefficient	Restless
Afraid	Dreamy	Inhibited	Sad
Alienated	Dumb	Insecure	Scattered
Ambivalent	Enraged	Irrational	Shy
Angry	Erratic	Irritable	Stimulated
Antagonistic	Euphoric	Isolated	Suspicious
Anxious	Excluded	Jealous	Tense
Apathetic	Exploited	Lethargic	Trusting
Apprehensive	Fearful	Lonely	Uncoordinated
Bitter	Forgetful	Maladjusted	Unhappy
Bored	Free	Melancholy	Unmotivated
Competitive	Frustrated	Moody	Unproductive
Compulsive	Giddy	Oppressed	Unreasonable
Confused	Gloomy	Paranoid	Unsociable
Defensive	Greedy	Passive	Unstable
Depressed	Guilty	Persecuted	Upset
Deprived	Hopeful	Preoccupied	Victimized
Despondent	Hopeless	Pressured	Vulnerable
Disappointed	Hostile	Rebellious	Withdrawn
Dissatisfied	Hurt	Regretful	Worried
	Hysterical	Rejected	

pressed, your limbs may feel heavy, lethargic, as if it takes enormous effort to move or think.

These are all physical sensations associated with particular feelings. Therefore, if you're having difficulty pinpointing exactly what your emotions are, it makes sense to stop a moment and examine what is happening on the physical level.

Below are some techniques you can use to help identify what you are feeling:

• Examine your bodily sensations and see what they tell you. Is there tension in your chest, or stomach. Are you having trouble breathing? Eating? Sleeping?

Do you feel all "revved up," or like a spring wound too tight? Would you like to hit someone, or throw something or break a cherished possession?

What do these physical sensations indicate to you about what you may be feeling?

• Write a letter to someone else, or to yourself, as in a diary. Just write down whatever you wish, anything that comes to mind. It might be about pressing concerns, worries, events, other people — whatever. Simply start writing and keep writing. As you write, again, notice your bodily sensations and notice the feelings that emerge along the way.

• Ask yourself if you have ever felt this same way before. Complete this sentence: The last time I felt like this was ⎯⎯⎯

⎯⎯⎯⎯⎯⎯⎯⎯⎯⎯⎯⎯⎯⎯⎯⎯⎯⎯⎯⎯⎯⎯⎯⎯⎯ .

Broaden your awareness of your feelings by remembering other times in your life when you felt the same way.

• Close your eyes and imagine yourself on a stage, telling the audience *exactly* how you feel about things. Don't pull any punches. Tell them everything, in explicit detail. Tell this audience of sympathetic listeners how wronged you have been, how hurt you are, or how angry. Curse fate, curse your offenders, curse whomever you feel like cursing. Even blame God if you want. Get your feelings out in this impassioned speech.

• Examine your behavior around others. Look at the way you are talking to your friends, your children, your spouse, or your co-workers. How are you acting toward them? Are you behaving testily, impatiently? Are you avoiding others, or covering up around them? Think about what you may be feeling when you're around other people.

• Finally, don't expect to feel the same as anyone else — even someone who is going through the same crisis. As we will see, how we feel emotionally depends primarily on how we evaluate the crisis event, what it means to us, how the event fits into our overall picture or image of life, and how it relates to our goals. These "meanings" are very private things, which means that the feelings accompanying a crisis can be very different, even among close family members.

The death of an eight-year-old girl, for example, is a tragic loss for her siblings, her parents, and her grandparents, as well as for neighbors, friends, school playmates, and teachers. Beyond this, however, feelings can be widely divergent. One brother might feel sad, but also guilty to still be alive himself; another brother might feel jealous of all the attention given his sister during her extended illness. The surviving parents may have their own unique feelings — anger, fear, or even relief, depending upon what the events have done to family life, each parent's hopes for the future, and their relationship with one another.

Express Your Feelings

Expressing your feelings simply means giving some kind of release to them. Expression can be verbal (talking them out) or nonverbal (acting them out).

One way is to go alone to a private room and close the door so you won't be overheard. Talk out loud to yourself; or pretend you are speaking to an invisible listener or an imaginary friend on the other end of a phone line. Tell this listener how you feel — *exactly* how you feel. Don't hold back. Curse, swear, rant and rave, or whatever, but give yourself to total communication with your imaginary listener.

Be careful not to interfere with the process by telling yourself, "This won't do any good" or "It won't change anything." True, raving, crying, getting angry, or whatever will not undo what has happened, but it can be critical to your personal recovery.

If talking to yourself makes you feel strange or uncomfortable, you can try to get a real live listener — a friend, a sympathetic family member, a counselor like a minister or priest. Anyone you think will be a good, unintruding listener.

Let the spotlight be on what you are feeling, not, at this point, what you are going to do about your situation. The main idea is simply to identify your reactions to the crisis, pin down your immediate feelings.

Talking to another person can be risky, however. Good listeners are hard to come by. The person who will allow you to express yourself without taking sides or judging your feelings or offering you unwanted advice is extremely rare. Most people do not know how to help by simply listening. But if you know someone who does, by all means talk to that person.

Another way to express hidden feelings is to write. Make a diary or journal, or write a long letter and fill it with all the things you are going through. Here again, don't hold back or try to be polite. Since you are not going to mail the letter it does not matter what you say. Be as angry, as hateful, or as depressed as you wish. You are only putting words on paper, and the paper does not matter. You are doing it for the release it brings.

Whether you choose to talk out your feelings or write them out, the main thing to remember is that by giving yourself to the task you can open channels within yourself that are usually closed. In opening them you can let your feelings begin to flow.

Another way to let feelings flow is through action. Some people, when angry, throw things or kick the dog. This is physical release of a sort, though with obvious disadvantages. You can try a similar, though much safer tactic.

Hitting a tennis ball, handball, or punching bag can bring release — especially if you picture the person or object causing your pain. In the same way, pounding your fists into pillows and giving words to your feelings is very effective. Don't be at all surprised at words or thoughts like "I hate you!" or "Don't ever do that again!" or "I won't take this anymore!" Therapists hear exclamations like this all the time as they encourage their clients to physically act out pent-up or frustrated emotions.

Let's sum up some ground rules for expressing feelings. The main "don'ts" of expressing feelings are these: (1) don't do things that will hurt living things (people, animals) and (2) don't yield to expressions that destroy property (cars, valuables, furniture).

The former is cruel; it can get you into trouble, and it will likely make your life much worse than it is right now. The latter is dangerous if not expensive, and there are better ways: talking, writing, hitting inert and inanimate objects (pillows, tennis balls, punching bags) are much more satisfying.

What we've said about expressing feelings may raise some questions for you: "Won't letting go and expressing things actually make matters worse? What if I stay angry, or stay upset. Shouldn't I resist it, not give in to it?"

Yes, harboring negative feelings can be unhealthy. Fanning the flames of anger, for example, nurturing bitterness, keeping pain at your side like a pet, or weeping as a lifestyle, are all destructive. This is not what we are talking about here. We are simply underlining the fact that identifying your feelings and then giving them some form of expression are necessary first steps in managing them. We also need to analyze these feelings (our next step) and control them — both of which will keep the "expression" part from getting out of hand.

Is all this "expressing emotions" simply a means of feeling sorry for yourself?

Maybe, maybe not. It really doesn't make any difference. Telling someone, "You are only feeling sorry for yourself" (or saying it to yourself) is usually a maneuver intended to stop the expression of feelings. Or, to stop some way of behaving that isn't considered acceptable — crying, for example.

Tears are usually considered a sign of weakness in Western society and are discouraged outright: "Crying only makes things worse" or "Tears won't solve anything," we are told. Tears, however, play a direct role in alleviating stress by releasing two important chemicals — leucine-enkephalin and prolactin — which are thought to be part of the body's supply of natural pain-relieving substances called endorphins.

These chemicals are present only in tears shed in response to emotion; tears resulting from some other cause, such as smoke or onions, do not contain the important pain-relievers. The presence of these natural substances may explain in part why it is that people feel better after a good cry: tears are a healthy response the body makes to help fight the stress of painful situations. Crying has very beneficial physical effects.

There is nothing wrong with feeling sorry for yourself for a while. If you have lost something very important to you, like a loved one, a friend, a relationship, a job, you have a right to your own tears of sympathy. Don't be inhibited by the notion that you are wallowing in your own pity or feeling sorry for yourself by crying. Cry anyway. It's one way you can take care of yourself.

Analyze Your Feelings
Once you have begun to get in touch with your feelings or can sense your emotions gaining release through expression, you can begin to analyze them. That is, you can begin to analyze the thoughts that go along with your painful feelings.

This sounds more difficult than it really is. Thoughts and feelings go together; they are interconnected in strange, often hidden, ways. As irrational as feelings can seem sometimes, there is a "sense" to them, though that sense may well be hidden at first.

Psychiatrist Arnold Beck has said that when we feel *depressed* it is an indication that we believe (a mental or cognitive process) we have lost something. An *anxious* feeling is an indication of a mental appraisal that we are being threatened in some way. A feeling of *anger* means we think an injustice has occurred to us or someone we care deeply about.

In other words, a feeling is an emotional reaction to a thought.

This is a very basic idea, but it serves a practical function in the process of learning to grow through a crisis. For, by finding out what you are *feeling,* you can get a glimpse into what you are *thinking,* which paves the way for making decisions about how to cope with the situation.

Usually, you will be completely unaware of this "appraisal" function because it most often takes place on a subconscious level. But through the conscious effort to express your feelings, you can begin to get insight into the thoughts behind them.

Insight might come in "flashes" — quick intuitive thoughts or images. Or it might come in the long, slow process of deliberately pondering over what you are feeling, seeking the thoughts behind the feelings.

Do you feel angry? Ask yourself, "Is there a particular face that comes to mind? A particular event?" "Have I been wronged?" "What is the injustice I am angry about?"

Do you feel depressed? Ask yourself, "What are my thoughts during this dark period?" "What have I lost?"

Here again, it may help to write down your feelings and thoughts. The idea is that right now, while feelings are being expressed, you should grab these insights, these images or thoughts, as they pass quickly through your mind.

The thoughts that go along with your feelings are important; do not ignore them. They will be extremely helpful to you later on. As stated earlier, your *feelings, thoughts,* and *behavior* are interconnected. By exploring your initial feelings and uncovering the thoughts behind them you will be able to learn what changes you will need to make to survive and grow through the crisis.

Control Your Feelings
This is the last step in managing painful feelings — learning to control your feelings. Control, not in the sense of burying

your feelings, but in the sense of not being controlled by them. There's a big difference.

What we are talking about here is employing specific remedies to help manage the impact of painful feelings. Control might come about through expression — "getting it all out." Or it might arise from other forms of management. There are at least four methods that can be used to help control painful feelings, to help keep them from overwhelming you.

1. *Counter painful feelings with exercise and relaxation techniques.* The techniques we discussed for physical survival in Chapter Five can be used to help control feelings as well.

Remember that, since feelings, thoughts, and behavior are inextricably linked together, a change in one will invariably bring about a change in another.

If you are anxious, for example, the anxiety is accompanied by physical tension: tight muscles in neck or stomach, clenched hands. This muscle tension manifests itself whenever you feel anxious; you feel anxious whenever you think about the event or situation that stirs up those feelings.

By manipulating the body — exercise, relaxation, deep breathing, yoga, and so on — you can change the effect of negative feelings. There is a growing body of literature that shows physical exercise can be an effective antidote to such strong feelings as depression, anxiety, and worry.

This is true at any time, but it can become critical during a crisis, and after. It is entirely appropriate during a crisis to combat the fearful, the wrenching, and the stressful, by working directly with your body.

2. *Invite laughter.* Your sense of humor can be an unexpected friend during a time of crisis.

The television show *M*A*S*H* has shown millions the lighter side of very dark situations. Often the point was made that there were times (and *are* times) when troubles are so bad the only thing to do is laugh. In the midst of all the pain, suffering, violence, and gore of war, for the surgeons and staff of the 4077th, often the only way to survive was to laugh.

Doris, a young lawyer, accepted a job at a top law firm in the city. And although she liked the competitive, "fast-track" atmosphere, she was scared most of the time, feeling that she was in way over her head. As a junior member of the firm, she had to put in long hours and undergo the exacting scrutiny of the senior members each time she prepared a case.

By the end of her fifth month she felt so tense that she was shouting at her secretary almost the minute she arrived at the office. The competition between the other junior members degenerated into free-for-all verbal sparring matches, which occasionally ended in real anger and frustration. But Doris was determined to succeed, and so she kept at it, despite real misgivings.

Her situation reached crisis proportions when her husband "attacked" her one evening, complaining that she was not paying enough attention to him. His job was not going all that well either, he told her; he needed her to help him keep his head on straight, but she had been neglecting him and their relationship. He accused her of loving her career more than she loved him.

That last accusation sent Doris fuming into the bedroom. She slammed the door, locked it, and threw herself on the bed. She was so angry that she looked for something to throw, saw a book on the nightstand, and grabbed it, thinking that she'd hurl it at the wall.

But the book was a Bible and she suddenly felt foolish holding a Bible in her hand and wanting to smash something with it. So, she sat down on the edge of the bed, flipped the Bible open, and began to read, thinking sarcastically, "Maybe there's something in here to help me."

A sentence caught her eye as she turned the pages: "Everything is meaningless!" What? Could that be right?

She read further: "All of it is meaningless, a chasing after the wind. I hated all the things I had toiled for under the sun."

"Oh, great," she mumbled under her breath. "That's some kind of encouragement." So far, the Bible didn't seem very comforting.

The top of the page read *Ecclesiastes;* Doris skipped on down and read some more: "What does a man get for all the toil and anxious striving . . . ?"

Toil and anxious striving, she thought, that's me.

"All his days his work is pain and grief . . ." Doris smiled in agreement; ". . . even at night his mind does not rest. This, too, is meaningless."

At this, Doris chuckled. She had turned to the Bible for comfort and the writer of the passage she found was just as depressed about life as she was! The thought made her laugh. She read some more and laughed louder.

"Hey, listen to this!" she called, emerging from the bedroom with the Bible in her hands. Her husband looked up, puzzled. "This guy is more depressed than I am!" Doris said.

She began reading to her husband and he laughed with her, immediately recognizing the way they had been acting for months. They laughed till it hurt, and the tension that had been building for weeks dissolved and flowed away.

This episode became a breakthrough for Doris. Though she still had problems at work, now, instead of flying off the handle or losing her cool when the situation got rough, she would simply remind herself of the grumpy philosopher of Ecclesiastes to regain her composure. "Everything is meaningless," she'd tell herself with a smile, "so don't take it personally."

Research suggests that laughter may indeed be one of the best medicines. Physically, laughter produces many of the same beneficial effects as exercise. Laughter is accompanied by increases in breathing rate, heart rate, and skin temperature in peripheral parts of the body.

Also, laughter increases the activity, tone, and metabolism of the body's muscles. Stanford University psychiatrist William F. Fry notes that blood pressure rises initially during laughter, and then drops below normal for one to two seconds afterwards. Studies indicate that the level of endorphins released from the brain increases during laughter, accounting for the sense of physical well-being people feel when they laugh. It has also been found that during laughter there is a general relaxation of other body muscles that are not directly involved in the process of laughter, leading to an overall release in tension.

But how can you "laugh at a time like this"?

Perhaps you can't. Don't force it. However, if humor emerges, even during your most painful times, don't shut it out. Think of humor and pain as two sides of the same coin — they *are* very much related. Your ability to laugh at some part of your plight can be a sign that you are beginning to gain new perspectives, new insights, which will guide you on the path toward healing. All of this is in addition to the fact that laughter is good for your body.

3. *Take a break from the crisis.* Sometimes the best move you can make is to get away from it all during a crisis. Going to a movie or going shopping for two or three hours might do wonders for your outlook.

Actually, anything is appropriate if it helps get your mind off the crisis for a time: reading an inspirational book, spending a few minutes alone in meditation or prayer, taking a walk in a quiet place, watching a TV show, or even packing a few things, leaving town for a weekend, and taking some time alone — there are innumerable ways of getting away from it all and, in the process, getting yourself in a better position for dealing positively with the crisis.

Many people, however, are reluctant to allow themselves this sort of brief vacation because they have a certain sense that, if they're not "working on it" full time, they are not playing by the rules.

But a crisis is not a game, and you do not have to play by the rules. Often, you need the brief respite that comes from taking a break.

4. *Put painful feelings in perspective: "This, too, shall pass."* Look ahead for a moment. Painful feelings will not last forever; nothing does. Your body and mind will not allow you to experience intense emotional pain for very long. Events go by. Feelings change. Thoughts change. Soon your body and mind will naturally begin regrouping and moving toward a new state of equilibrium.

Look back as well. Ask yourself: "When was the last time I felt like this?"

Explore it a little. Have you felt this way before? When? What were the circumstances? What were you doing? How old were you? What happened to make you feel that way?

It may be that the crisis event is so devastating, so explosive, that the feelings it unleashes are totally and completely new to you. The threat or danger you experience is so great that you feel anxiety more intensely than you have ever felt it before. The loss may be so severe that you are depressed beyond all belief. Or the injustice so overwhelming that it dwarfs anything you ever imagined possible.

Then again, the feelings, as intense and painful as they are, may be very much like those you felt at an earlier time in life. In some cases the intensity of the current crisis ties directly to the fact that it dredges up *old* feelings — you are now experiencing the pain of the current crisis *and* the pain of a previous crisis all at the same time.

Indeed, this is often what makes it so hard to cope. If you are going through a divorce, for example, your present feelings may remind you of the deep rejection you felt when you lost a sweetheart in high school. If you lose a job, it might conjure up the same feelings you experienced when you were cut from the school team. Your emotional reaction to a traumatic injury may stir up the same feelings that you had when your parents were divorced when you were a child.

Depending upon your earlier experiences, the crisis event may trigger any number of different feelings inside you.

Here is where putting your feelings in perspective with the rest of your life can help. For if you are able to establish a connection between the crisis now and an earlier crisis, perhaps long past, you can view your present situation with less alarm. After all, you *did* survive the previous crisis — you are still here! You can make it through this one, too.

Remember, also, the built-in opportunity that exists whenever something from the past — an old, unfinished crisis — is stirred up again. New growth is possible. Perhaps now, once and for all, you can rework old events, understand recurring feelings, express them, and come out stronger than you were before.

In other words, you can break the bonds of the past. That painful experience may never hold the same pain for you that it has held up to now. The next chapter will tell you how to examine these old ghosts and lay them to rest. You can rework the past, so to speak, by confronting past issues that have been hurting you, perhaps subconsciously. Now you can clean the slate for good.

THE PARADOX

Of the four steps we've been discussing — identifying, expressing, analyzing, and controlling feelings — you may have noticed what seems like a contradiction in our emphasis on both *expressing* and *controlling* painful feelings. The fact is that there is a time and a place for each.

Neither one is more important than the other. Both need to happen.

There will be times when you need to express your feelings and other times when control is necessary. Over the course of the weeks and months to follow you will experience this paradox — expressing them when you most feel like controlling them and controlling them when you may feel more like expressing them.

It might help if you think of your painful feelings as a rudder. It can steer both ways — too far to the right toward control (keeping a tight rein on your emotions) and it must be balanced by a correction to the left toward expression (letting loose a little). That's how you keep on course.

Remember, you are not interested in dominating your feelings or getting them over with. Your goal is to manage them just enough to allow you to begin moving ahead on the next two steps of crisis resolution: changing your mind and adjusting your behavior. When these are accomplished, your painful feelings will become even more manageable.

IT'S NATURAL

What we have been describing in this chapter is another aspect of the phoenix factor — the very natural path that survivors follow to lead them out of a crisis.

Your own instincts will probably have confirmed that the steps we have described are true. For example, when a crisis strikes, it's natural to have intense feelings churning around inside you and to recognize them. This is what we mean by identifying them — you ask yourself, "What am I feeling? What is going on inside me?"

Next, you will normally give some sort of expression to what you are feeling. Instead of bottling up your emotions, ignoring them, or tucking them away in some dark corner somewhere, you might say to yourself, "I feel terrible, I've got to let some of this out!" You do — in appropriate ways — release the pressure and tension you feel in keeping the emotions inside. You jog, play tennis, work in the garden, walk around the block, talk to a good friend, cry — anything to let off steam. It is natural to do this.

Having gotten some of the feelings out in the open, it makes sense to ask yourself what they mean: "What's going on here? What are my feelings trying to tell me?" Again, this is a very normal and natural thing to do. As a survivor, you do not run from your feelings; instead you delve into them a bit and see what you can learn about yourself that will help you now and in the future. You let your feelings become a beacon to point you toward growth.

Finally, there comes a time when you have to put your feelings aside — you can't go on wallowing in the pain forever. There is work to be done, children to care for, tasks to be attended to. Feelings, natural though they may be, cannot be allowed to take over life completely. So, you corral them and exert a little control over them; you take a break from the crisis and exercise, or laugh, or just get on with life, reminding yourself that the crisis is, after all, only temporary — it will pass.

This is the normal and natural way that survivors manage the emotional aspect of a crisis. In fact, you will discover this process for yourself *if* you don't interfere with it. The suggestions in this chapter have been given to alert you to this process, so that you will not accidentally block the natural path toward healing and growth, and to show you how to get it "unblocked" if you find yourself stuck along the way.

Again, the steps themselves are simple:
— Identify your feelings
— Express them in acceptable ways
— Analyze their meaning
— Control their potentially negative effects
Remember, even the most painful feelings can be used to your advantage. Your feelings can be a beacon in the night, pointing a way toward healing and growth.

• SEVEN •

Changing Your Mind

BOB'S WORLD fell apart when his parents got divorced. The boy was thirteen at the time and recalled later that before the divorce he had always held his father, a very ambitious man, on a pedestal, idolizing the way his father walked, talked, worked, everything. But when his parents announced their separation, Bob found out that the reason for the divorce was that his father had been seeing another woman. Not all the time that his father had spent "on the road" had been for business trips.

Bob thought he had forgotten all of this, but it came to mind fifteen years later when he was filling out a life history questionnaire given him by a therapist. Bob had sought counseling because he was lacking direction in his life — working in a dead-end job he felt was going nowhere, but didn't know what to do about it.

When asked about his goals, he recalled that he hadn't had any for a long time — all the way back to when his parents were divorced. Before then, he remembered, he had been tremendously ambitious. But when Bob's father fell off the pedestal, Bob grew listless and indifferent. He reasoned that, since his father had cruelly lied to his mother, such dishonesty cast suspicion on everything his father had taught him. His father was a hypocrite, not to be believed anymore about anything.

Bob became the resident teenage cynic, telling everyone that adults were never to be trusted. With no one to look up to, he quit trying to find any direction for his life and instead spent most of his time and energy criticizing adults.

Jane was visiting her cousin for a week or two while she found an apartment of her own, and a job, in the city. She had always been close to her cousin and very friendly with her cousin's husband. One day, while Jane's cousin was away at work, the husband came home early. One thing led to another, and before she knew it she was involved in a two-day affair with a married man.

She felt guilty enough about what was happening to break it off, and without saying anything to anyone, she got an apartment of her own and moved out.

The episode was over, but Jane continued to be plagued with guilt about what she had done. She tried to minimize or downplay her sexual feelings when she went out with other men. Jane realized that in the eyes of her church what she had done was sinful, but she didn't know what to do to get past what had happened. She tried to forget about it, and eventually succeeded.

Three years later, however, she got married and immediately began having sexual problems in her marriage. Unable to relax, she found little enjoyment in sex. She attempted to make sex a much smaller part of her life than her husband was comfortable with. After months of frustration they sought guidance from their physician, hoping he could help.

THINKING ANIMALS

These two cases have a common theme: Both Bob and Jane formed conclusions about themselves and about the world based on what happened to them during a crisis. The conclusions changed their lives in the future. The problem is that what they concluded was erroneous.

In Bob's case, he could not square the fact of his father's infidelity with an image of his father as a man who was perfect. Upon discovering a flaw, he mistakenly concluded that all adults were hypocrites and never to be trusted.

For Jane, her two-day affair was a cardinal sin, one that could not be forgiven. She concluded that because she had sinned, she did not have a right to happiness. As punishment she began to close off sexually.

Carl Sagan reminds us in his TV series *Cosmos* that we are "thinking animals" — this is what makes us different from all other creatures on this planet. Because of our brains we are the masters of the earth. This mastery is all important to the survival of the human species, and to the well-being of the individual as well. It is a fact that the people who do not resolve a crisis successfully are usually those who have not mastered the crisis mentally.

Mastering the crisis mentally is the heart of crisis resolution. How you interpret the crisis event, how you understand it, and what you conclude about it all have a powerful effect on the rest of your life.

If you believe that as a result of the crisis you are no longer worthy of love, you will tend to see yourself as unlovable. If you believe that you have been victimized unfairly, you will see yourself as a victim, and you will feel like a victim.

What you believe about yourself affects not only your feelings about yourself but the way you act, too. That is why a crisis seems to tear out whole chunks of life and scatter the pieces. The crisis event goes against what we always thought life was like; it strikes at our basic beliefs and shatters our picture of life, our expectations of life.

This gap between what has just happened (the crisis event) and what you always thought life was about (your mental picture) is the heart of the problem. In this chapter we will examine not only what happened, but how to interpret it — all with a view to finding a way of looking at the world that explains what has happened and equips you to grow.

CHANGING YOUR MIND

In the last chapter we talked about how the feelings of depression, sadness, anger, bitterness, and all the rest are tied to how we think about or interpret a particular situation. And where managing the painful feelings of a crisis means uncovering them if they are hidden and expressing them in productive ways, "changing your mind" strikes at the interpretation aspect of the crisis situation.

The process of changing your mind has two aims: (1) to help you understand how you are thinking about the crisis and (2) to adjust attitudes, to amend or change beliefs, in order to insure growth through the crisis. That is what it means to change your mind.

From the very beginning in this book, we have proclaimed the opportunity for growth that can occur through crisis. When the flames of crisis threaten to consume everything — life has a chance to become new. New directions can be chosen; old, unfinished issues (neurotic hang-ups, some call them) from the past resurface in unexpected ways so that you have a chance to rework them and finish them once and for all. This is the opportunity side of every crisis — the chance for rebirth and growth, which is the main theme of this book.

It so happens that reworking past issues and choosing new directions are primarily mental tasks — involving memories from childhood, the way you think about your parents, about the world, God, the universe, and your place in it.

In learning how to change your mind, you will be learning how to reckon with these thoughts, memories, and images in such a way that you can revise them in light of the crisis and change them to allow you to face the future in a stronger, healthier position.

DO YOU KNOW WHAT HAPPENED?

Rick, a cabinetmaker, had just opened a shop of his own, something he had been dreaming about for a long time. He was very happy and spent long hours every day designing and building fine cabinetry. One day, however, just a few minutes before quitting time, he hurried through a last cut on his large table saw. The next thing Rick knew, the saw blade snagged and drew his hand into the blade, severing three fingers.

Rick was rushed to the hospital, where his fingers were painstakingly rejoined. Still, the damage had been done; he lost the use of his fingers and was forced to give up his shop. He sold his tools to another cabinetmaker and entered another profession.

Later, in the course of working through this crisis, Rick was plagued with unanswered questions. Why did this happen? Was the blade faulty? Was I having a bad day? Was I thinking of something else when I should have been watching my work? Was I just careless? Was this a sign of my incompetence?

These questions are not irrelevant. How Rick interprets his accident — what it means to him — will be all important in how he resolves the crisis. In order to resolve the crisis of physical injury and disability, it will be necessary for Rick to find answers to his questions. In order to grow, Rick will have to understand what has happened — and why.

All crisis events are dramatic confrontations with how we view ourselves. A crisis either radically confirms or radically challenges something we have always believed about ourselves and our lives.

Sometimes the crisis confirms a bad self-image. In Rick's case the accident might reaffirm his image of himself as clumsy or inept or "doomed to failure." If he comes away from the accident judging himself as a total incompetent, a failure at everything he tries, or viewing it as God's punishment for human error, real growth is going to be very difficult.

Or perhaps the crisis comes as a powerful challenge to a particular view of ourselves — it is so contradictory to our self-image that we can't handle the dissonance. Using Rick's case once again, maybe Rick had always considered himself the living example of safety, priding himself on his care and skill with power tools. He saw himself as a master craftsman — always in control, always precise in his movements, with each step carefully thought out. His accident challenges that picture — destroys it, in fact. In this situation, then, Rick's crisis stems from the fact that his belief about himself is in direct conflict with the facts of his accident.

Either way — whether the crisis comes as a confirmation or a challenge — we are left with a lot of questions that need answers: How could this happen? Why me? What did I do? What does this mean?

Finding answers to these questions is the first step toward gaining what counselors call "cognitive mastery" over the crisis. That is, gaining mental control over the event — understanding what happened and what it means to you.

Comprehending what has happened is sometimes a difficult process to undertake. It requires an unflinching look at the realities of the situation, which is often far from pleasant.

In divorce, death, loss of job, illness, disability, natural disaster, or any other cause of crisis, there are many unpleasant aspects of the situation — realities, facts, objective data. It is normal to feel fearful in facing unpleasant facts, for it could well mean facing an unpleasant truth about yourself.

For Rick, the cabinetmaker, to achieve understanding and mastery of the situation meant that he had to face the fact that it might not have been a faulty blade, as he first suspected, but that his injury might well be due to his own negligence.

Rick eventually had to push past his fear of facing facts in order to develop a reality-based understanding of what happened. Once past his negative feelings about facing the facts — depression over his carelessness and guilt about what he'd done to himself — Rick could begin moving toward growth.

Negative feelings alone, no matter how powerful, cannot harm you. It is not the end of the world to face facts and get upset over what happened. As a matter of fact, it is the beginning of healing — a little like lancing a boil is the beginning of recovery, painful though it might be.

Find Out What Happened

Sometimes the process of understanding what happened will require that you get more information. It may mean simply reviewing what happened and talking about it with a friend, your spouse, or a counselor. Other times, however, you may need to do a little detective work to get all the facts. You may need to go to people involved in the crisis — a parent, a boss, a police officer, a doctor, or a minister, depending upon the nature of the crisis and others involved.

Cal returned home late one night to a ringing telephone. Upon answering it, he was informed by a police officer that his brother Ray had died as a result of a drug overdose. Although Cal knew his brother had smoked a little marijuana in college, he had no idea that Ray had been using harder drugs. The midnight call came as a devastating shock to Cal.

That night he could not sleep. He kept hearing the awful words of the policeman in his head: "Found dead in a motel room . . . lethal overdose . . . next of kin . . ." Picturing his brother on the floor of a cheap motel room, with a needle in his vein, Cal's mind filled with a million questions. Was it a mistake? How could such a thing happen to Ray? What about Ray's job as a high-level computer designer? How was it possible?

After the funeral, Cal could not escape the questions that

haunted him. He realized he had to get the answers if he was ever to understand his brother's death. So, boarding a plane, Cal flew to San Francisco where Ray had been living, and he began talking to some of the people who had known his brother. He talked to the police officer who had called him and to the motel owner who had found his brother's body. The owner showed him the room where his brother had stayed and gave him a box containing Ray's belongings — mostly drug-related paraphernalia.

Ray's friends told Cal that his brother had begun using harder drugs more heavily of late, after being fired from a very promising position with a computer company. He had been too embarrassed to let his family know about his dependency and his failure at work. Unable to bring himself to ask for help, Ray recklessly ended his life in an overdose.

Cal returned home saddened by what he learned but with the knowledge that he was beginning to find missing pieces to the puzzle of his brother's death. The tragic death was less of a mystery now that Cal faced the fact of his brother's involvement with drugs and how they had ended his life.

In any crisis situation it is extremely important not only to understand what happened and why, but to know the truth about what happened, however unpleasant that might be. Getting at the truth is the key to this finding-out process.

You can begin by asking yourself these questions:

"How much do I know about what really happened?"

"What questions do I have?"

"Are there gaps in my information?"

"How can I get this information?"

It may be that early in the crisis you will not want a lot of information. But that could change as time goes on. Research indicates that people do vary in the amount of information they require in order to satisfactorily understand a situation. If you are a person who likes to face facts head on, chances are you'll want all the details you can get. On the other hand, you may not want details at all — a more general overview of what happened is all you require.

Either way, in answering the suggested questions, you will map out for yourself the areas where you may require more factual information and where you can find it. Then follow through, and get to the truth of what happened.

Some people avoid facing the facts of a crisis because it makes them feel uncomfortable. They fear the truth and what it might reveal about themselves. The truth can often be unpleasant.

What man would enjoy reviewing the course of his marriage, for example, and discovering that it failed because he had been acting like a jerk all along, or finding out that his incompetence on the job led to his getting fired? What woman would care to face the fact that her relentlessly pessimistic attitude drove her husband away?

These realizations — unpleasant as they are — do not kill. No one is harmed facing the truth, although there might be a tremendous amount of pain involved at the time. If, however, facing the truth is avoided out of fear for the pain involved, worse things can happen — future growth can be stunted or halted altogether.

Survivors of life crises regularly report that it was only in facing some painful truth that they were able to open the door to the future, to make changes and correct errors of the past.

Find Out What It Means

The first step toward mental mastery of the crisis is to find out what happened and why, to get to the facts of the incident and face the truth. Step two is to find out what the event *means*.

Lloyd had been having difficulty controlling Andy, his oldest son. The boy, seventeen, had a mind of his own and resented anything Lloyd said to him, refusing to acknowledge his father's authority over him. One morning, after Andy had failed to come home the night before, Lloyd confronted him

about his careless behavior. The two fought, and Lloyd, or-
dinarily a passive man, struck his son and knocked him down.
Andy stormed out of the house, vowing never to return.

Two days and two nights passed and Andy did not show
up. Lloyd became frantic, imagining all sorts of horrible
things had happened to his son. He called all of Andy's friends
and asked them about the boy, but none of them admitted
seeing him or knowing where he was. After two days, Lloyd
called the police and told them Andy had run away. The police
officer who took his call brusquely informed him that there
was little they could do, that they simply had too many runaway reports to deal with individual cases, and that he should
have kept his son under better control.

As weeks passed, and still no word from Andy, Lloyd grew
more and more anxious. He could not concentrate on his
work, and spent every evening driving downtown trying to
find his son. He put ads in the paper and circulated pictures
of his son to all the newspapers and put them on bulletin
boards throughout the city, but Andy never called.

Lloyd felt he had lost his son forever, that he had failed as
a father and was now being punished for spending so much
time at work when Andy was growing up. He thought that
everyone was sneering at him behind his back because he
could not keep his own son in line. He believed that he and
Andy would never be able to get back together now, that all
hope of a future relationship was gone. He imagined Andy
somewhere laughing at him for being such a worthless father.

Was Lloyd correct? Was his assessment of himself as a father
true? Actually, Lloyd was quite wrong about several of his beliefs. But that didn't make much difference in how he felt —
true or not, he believed them just the same and felt terrible
because of it. Lloyd was out of touch with reality where his
son was concerned, and it was poisoning his life.

It was only when he began to examine his false beliefs —
that he had been a bad father, that all hope of reconciliation

was lost, that people thought less of him for having trouble with his son — only when Lloyd held these false beliefs up to the clear light of reality did he see how wrong he had been.

The reality was that Andy's leaving exposed deep-seated problems in both father and son, and in their relationship. The fist fight was the last straw. Andy had been having problems relating to authority long before the fight. Lloyd later discovered that his faulty perception of the situation was due to an old fear that he was unworthy of raising a son — a fear that had haunted him often in early fatherhood. Andy's leaving confirmed this fear for him; it meant that he had indeed failed and was an unworthy father.

How do you go about discovering the meaning of a crisis? One way to start is by simply asking yourself: "Do I know what this crisis event really means to me?"

This question brings you to the heart of the crisis. For, as we will see, the *facts* of an event are distinctly different from the *meaning* of an event. The facts cannot change; the meaning or interpretation of an event can. Sometimes it is important for growth that the meaning does change. This is part of what we mean when we talk about *changing your mind.*

Another way of finding out what a crisis event means is to ask: "How do I interpret the crisis?"

Rick, in a previous example, might have asked himself: What does my cutting off three fingers in the saw mean? Does that mean I'm incompetent? Does it mean I'm a failure? Am I less of a person now that I'm partially disabled? Does it challenge my previous view of myself as a person who never makes mistakes? Does it reinforce my attitude that I'm careless and accident prone?

In the same way, a woman who had a mastectomy might ask herself: Am I less of a woman? Am I now unattractive sexually? Do I believe that I am doomed to an unfulfilling sex life?

A person recently divorced might discover what the crisis means by asking: Does it mean that I have forfeited my right to happiness forever? Does it mean I'm sinful? Does it mean I am destined to fail at every relationship?

Lloyd, the father of the runaway, might ask himself: Was Andy's leaving proof of my failure? Does it mean that I have no right to consider myself a good father? Is this a punishment for not doing more for him as a child? Am I an unworthy parent?

In each case there was an objective, factual event — an injury, a surgery, a divorce, a runaway child. In each case the objective, factual event was followed by subjective interpretations or evaluations of the event — I am a failure, I am ruined, I am sinful, I am unworthy. These evaluations or interpretations are what we *believe* about the event. They are not the event itself.

This is an important point, because for many people the difference between the *facts* of the event and their *beliefs* about the event is not at all easy to distinguish. But broken down it might look something like this:

FACT: I was fired from my job.

BELIEF: This means I am incompetent.

Often, because of the way you perceive yourself and the world around you, facts and beliefs mingle and meld together and become extremely difficult to untangle. But the separation of facts from beliefs must take place.

The meaning of a crisis event for you may not always please you. What you find out may well be embarrassing; your interpretation could cause some discomfort to you. It might seem childish, or absurd, or just plain crazy.

Everyone has embarrassing, childish, crazy, or irrational thoughts; and facing them, admitting them, if only to oneself, is the first step toward getting rid of them. The point to remember is that the thought or belief — no matter how childish or irrational — is the link between what you feel right now and how you will feel and act in the future. To begin gaining an understanding of what the crisis means, you must grab hold of those thoughts or images or beliefs and expose them to the light of your own awareness.

YOUR PROGRAM

Perhaps one way to begin understanding the difference between the facts of an event and beliefs about that event is to recognize that all of us carry a sort of computer program in our heads. This program is our design of life and is usually very helpful in many ways — it allows us to make decisions, gives us direction for the future, enables us to predict or to anticipate the normal occurrences of life. How tedious life would be if, every morning, we had to stop and rethink the entire process of getting up, getting dressed, and going to work. We do it without thinking about it once that process has been added to our program.

But a crisis tears big holes in the program. By definition, a crisis means that the program of life has been damaged in one way or another. The crisis event can:

1. Violate one of my major expectations about life
2. Produce terrifying or frightening images
3. Expose weaknesses or cognitive errors in my mental program
4. Contradict one of my "big beliefs" — religious or philosophical assumptions
5. Drag up unfinished business from the past
6. Show that I am working with the wrong program
7. Combine with other stressors to "overload the circuits," leading to a complete breakdown

Understanding how a crisis wreaks havoc with your internal program can help you take the necessary first steps toward the goal of changing your mind, that is, gaining mental control of the crisis. Let's examine in more detail each of the ways a crisis can ruin your program.

The Event Violates One of My Major Expectations About Life

You go through life with very definite ideas about the way life is, the way it ought to be, and the way it will turn out for you. A crisis often jars this expectation; it violates the way you view life, often to such an extent you believe you cannot go on living. The signs that your expectations have been shattered are statements like:

"I can't believe this is happening . . ."
"I can't accept this . . ."
"It's just impossible that . . ."
"I can't imagine how . . ."

Each of these statements indicates that the crisis event is sharply at odds with the way you believe the world should be. There are several major categories of expectations that can be violated during a crisis.

Marriage. You might have very concrete ideas about what your marriage should be like, how long it should last, fidelity to/from your marriage partner. Divorce, death, or infidelity can explode those views.

Careers. You might have a certain picture in mind of what your working life should be like, the respect you should receive, success you will attain, how long it will take you to succeed. Getting fired or laid off can destroy the picture you've painted for yourself. In the same way, a man who dreams of becoming president of the company by the time he's forty-five might suffer a severe blow when he reaches his forty-fifth birthday with no such promotion in sight.

Length and quality of life. You might have an expectation about how long you will live. Maybe you see yourself living out your days happily and productively to a ripe old age, surrounded by loving friends and family. News about a terminal illness or an accident resulting in physical disability can dramatically alter your expectation.

Most people are not at all aware of just how concrete their expectations are until a crisis crashes headlong into them. These life expectations, and the timetables to go with them, are developed through contact with various sources; we get them from parents, through education, church, books we read, magazines, and television. As we go through life we develop very definite ideas about who we are, what our futures will be like, what kind of material possessions we will have, the relationships we will develop, and so on.

Our expectations become just as much a part of us as a hand or a foot. Losing even one is never easy. During a crisis, however, *all* major expectations may be violated.

> • John always thought he'd be a lawyer. His father is a judge; his mother is a lawyer, as are his older brother and an uncle. In fact, he has never considered that he would be anything *but* a lawyer. John, however, cannot get into law school — his grades are just not good enough to be accepted. His LSAT scores completely rule out law school as a viable option.

> • Martha and her husband dreamed of the time when he would sell his dry-cleaning shop and they would move up to their cabin in the northern part

of Wisconsin. She always pictured herself walking hand-in-hand with her husband into the sunset years. But her husband died of a heart ailment at the age of fifty-three, and she is left to run the dry cleaners by herself.

What happened in these two examples is easy to see — a major life expectation has been violated. It makes no difference that one is merely a failure to get into law school while the other is the loss of a life mate; one is not worse than the other because death is concerned. Each is a crisis event for the individual experiencing it.

In order to deal with the crisis effectively, you must find out what your expectations were *before* the crisis event and how these expectations have been damaged by what has happened. You must ask yourself, "What expectations have been violated?"

The answer may not come readily; you may have to spend some time thinking about it, listening to yourself, expressing yourself, talking to others. But when it comes, the answer will appear in a form something like this:

"I see that what is so devastating about this right now is that I never thought it could happen to me. Things like this just happen to others. I always thought my life would be as I pictured it. Now everything's changed."

This is the most helpful and direct way to deal with shattered expectations — to identify them as just that: expectations that have been damaged, instead of something bigger, such as "My life is ruined forever!" or "All hope for the future is lost!"

You are a complex person with thoughts, feelings, behavior, physical attributes. You are more than your expectations. Take hope from the fact that right now, as a result of a severe blow, you are dealing with only *one* aspect of your life — your expectations — not all of your complex being.

You will approach the job of rebuilding in much better condition if you recognize that you are rebuilding a *view* of life, not life itself — a view of life based on previous expectations that have been torn down.

Survivors eventually replace shattered expectations with new beliefs, new expectations. The young man who failed to get into law school finds a new view of life that does not depend upon his becoming a lawyer. The woman whose husband died discovers a new image of herself as a single person who can make it on her own. The cabinetmaker who cut his fingers begins to see himself in a role of something other than a man who works with his hands.

The Event Produces Frightening Thoughts or Images

In some cases the crisis is touched off by some very traumatic event — a horrible disaster that results in death or great physical suffering for victims. A flood, fire, tornado, or the terror of a rape or murder may leave survivors shaken and haunted by vivid images of what happened. Sometimes these images can be overwhelming — as if one is reliving the event all over again.

Even the most frightening images and thoughts about past events will subside in time if you allow yourself to express the feelings that go along with them, as we discussed in the previous chapter. Therefore, the direct treatment for painful images is to talk about them with an individual who is willing to listen.

Experience with Vietnam veterans who were victims of post-traumatic stress disorder bore this out. What many veterans found when they returned was that they could not forget the agony they had seen in war; they were haunted by daydreams and nightmares of horrible war images — sometimes for years after the event.

The best treatment for freeing these veterans from their painful images and thoughts has been for them to be able to talk about their memories with other veterans and with counselors who have had similar war experiences — people who understood and did not judge, but simply listened.

What happens is that in talking about painful images you become desensitized to what happened. Once it is told, a horrible image cannot have the same shock value as before. Some therapists ask clients to "tell me the story" about what happened. And then after the story has been told, they say, "Tell me the story again." Releasing yourself from the hold of the images and memories is a matter of allowing the images to come out, letting the painful thoughts surface.

You can do this by yourself, with a friend you can trust simply to listen, or with a counselor who will allow you to talk freely. Talking about what happened and your images of it — along with the passage of time — will heal.

The Event Exposes Weaknesses or Errors in My Mental Program

Many sources — parents, education, religious beliefs, books, the media, and so on — contribute to your program for life. Since it is drawn from so many different, often contradictory, sources, it is not surprising when the program contains a few errors. A crisis can critically expose such weaknesses or errors.

You, like everyone else around you, may carry with you unrealistic goals or ideals for both yourself and others. Often a crisis will point out just how irrational some of these ideals or beliefs can be. The error might be a misconception about yourself, the world, your goals. Generally, these things are tucked away somewhere in the subconscious. During a crisis, they come out and occupy center stage.

Many people carry around a self-defeating notion or two, such as "I must be loved and admired by everyone" or "I must never offend anyone" or "I must be perfect at all times and in all ways to be a worthwhile person." No one, of course, would say these things in so many words, yet people believe them and behave accordingly. Obviously, it is impossible to be loved by everyone you meet, just as it is impossible to be perfect and never offend anyone. If you have been living your life according to these unspoken ideals, it has probably gotten you into trouble in one way or another.

You may, for example, have put too much energy and time into certain relationships that can never be what you want them to be. Or you may feel that you cannot let a project go until it is just right. The only problem is that you never can get it "just right," so you tend to turn things in late, never finish them at all, or, worse, never even start them.

As remarkable as it might sound, this is where a crisis can actually be advantageous; it offers an opportunity to make a significant and freeing change. For many people, living with unrealistic standards is something that they get by with because the irrational belief is never put to the test. The crisis, however, breaks everything down, exposing the fact that the unrealistic belief won't carry you along anymore.

Linda was a perfectionist in all her activities as a wife and mother. She kept her house spotless, never served a meal late, worked on committees at church and at her children's school, was deeply involved in many civic affairs, prided herself on being a caring and conscientious friend to her neighbors — in short, tried to be all things to all people.

She was so busy all the time, juggling her many responsibilities while trying to raise two bright kids and keep her husband happy, that she was often frustrated and physically exhausted because of spreading herself too thin. Still, she was never able to give up any of her commitments, or lower her standards, because that would be a sign of imperfection on her part. She believed that in order to satisfy her husband she had to be the perfect wife; the moment she let down he would leave her.

A crisis came for Linda when her husband, realizing what she was doing to herself, finally told her that if she did not slow down and give up some of her responsibilities he *would* leave her. She became furious, thinking, "How can that man say such a thing! I've been working so hard to be the perfect wife for him. What does he want from me?"

Linda took his comment as a criticism of her and her anger threw her into a frenzy of activity. She assumed more jobs and responsibilities than before, while simultaneously maintaining her household even more rigorously. Before long, her health gave out and she collapsed in nervous exhaustion, winding up with a long stay in the hospital.

While she was hospitalized Linda had time to think, and although she feared that things would just go to pieces in her absence, she also found it restful not to have to worry about every little detail of all her involvements. When she saw that the world did indeed go on without her — her children still got to school in clean clothes, meals were still cooked, the various boards and committees she served on still functioned, people could take care of themselves without her intervention — Linda began to relax for the first time in years.

She also discovered that her irrational perfectionism had been triggered by a conversation she had had with her mother-in-law prior to her marriage. Her husband's mother had told her, "Jim can't stand a messy house; he's just like his dad — if supper is a minute late he blows his top. I guess that's why we're divorced. I never could manage to live up to his idea of perfection." Linda believed that in order to keep her marriage together she had to be perfect, and yet it was this irrational belief that was ruining her and sabotaging her marriage.

If you look closely at a crisis, you may find that the intensity of the pain is often directly related to some irrational belief that has been exposed by an explosive event.

For example, it is usually painful if a man gets fired from his job. But if the man who gets fired has believed that he must never make a mistake and never fail, then the event of getting fired is not simply a problem of unemployment to be faced, but rather a full-blown life crisis: now the whole world can see that the man who had to be perfect isn't perfect at all, the man who could not fail has failed.

In order to correct warped views, irrational beliefs, faulty ideals — these weaknesses in our programs — it is first necessary to identify the distortion in the thinking process. Next, the distorted thoughts must be replaced with a better balanced, more truthful, conception and interpretation of the facts. Finally, the new view must be practiced daily until it becomes as much a habit, as much a part of the program, as the old distorted view.

Researchers Hammond and Stanfield have developed a list of various distorted beliefs. Scan the list below and see which ones apply to you.

1. Distorted Self-Definitions
   a. I am a helpless, innocent victim. Unhappiness and what occurs in life are caused by outside circumstances or past events for which I am not responsible and have no control.
   b. I am not attractive, feminine (or manly) enough.
   c. I am deficient (for example, not smart enough) and therefore destined to fail.
   d. I am wicked.
   e. I am weak (and need to be led).
   f. I am so exceptional that I am entitled to my own way (narcissistic entitlement).
   g. I am undesirable and no one could love me.
   h. My worth is measured by my performance.
   i. I am worthless if my spouse (girlfriend, boyfriend, mother, father, child) does not love me.

2. Mistaken Assumptions About People and the World

   a. Life is a dangerous, dog-eat-dog jungle. (People are hostile competitors.)

   b. Life doesn't give me a chance, and I'm destined to fail.

   c. Men (women) cannot be trusted.

   d. Life is chaotic and completely unpredictable.

   e. People are stupid, and one ought to take them for all he/she can.

   f. Other people are happy, "normal," and do not have feelings or problems similar to mine. In fact, some people have perfect marriages, perfect children, ideal jobs, and so on.

   g. Good looks, superior intelligence, athletic ability, money, and so forth make one happy.

   h. People will look down on me as inept if I make or admit mistakes, admit limitations, and seek advice.

   i. Most things are either black or white, that is, good or bad, right or wrong, liked or disliked, clever or stupid, attractive or unattractive.

3. Mistaken, Self-Defeating Goals

   a. It is essential to be perfect, completely competent and without flaw to be worthwhile. Don't make or admit mistakes.

   b. I must be loved and approved of (admired, liked) by everyone. I must never offend.

   c. I must find the perfect or "right" solution.

   d. I have to be the best, the first, or right.

   e. I must be the center of attention, the star attraction.

   f. I must be dependent on someone stronger to protect and lead me.

   g. I should retaliate and get even with the world.

   h. I must not let people know what I am really like (they may think less of me or use what they learn against me).

i. I must ventilate anger whenever I feel it.

j. I must be safe and secure at all times. I must be careful not to take any risks or chances.

k. I must be completely self-sufficient and independent.

4. Mistaken Ideals

a. The only thing worth being is a "star" (or genius). Nothing less is worth working for.

b. I should always be cool, calm, and collected and never lose control.

c. I should always know the right answer.

d. I should be the perfect spouse, parent, lover, employee, son, daughter, church member, and so on.

e. A "real" man is a tough guy who never takes any guff from anyone.

f. A "real" woman should always be "feminine," inoffensive, unassertive, and dependent.

g. I should always have my own way.

h. I have an easier and happier life when I avoid responsibilities and problems.

i. I should be able to succeed and be happy without discomfort or struggle.

j. I should always be unselfish, considerate, generous, happy.

k. The purpose of life is to work hard and to be productive — not happy.

l. If you try hard enough you can excel at anything and everything.*

If you have identified an error in your program, you can begin to correct it by telling yourself that it is time to erase it.

*From D. C. Hammond and K. Stanfield, *Multidimensional Psychotherapy: A Counselors' Guide for the MAP Form* (Champaign, Ill.: Institute for Personality and Ability Testing, 1977). Reprinted by permission.

There is no better time than right now. The sooner you're free of the erroneous belief the sooner you can begin dealing with life in a more balanced, realistic way.

Start by replacing the old, distorted view with the truth. If you identified yourself by the statement "I am deficient and therefore destined to fail," replace it with a statement like "I am proficient in many areas, though not in all areas. My success or failure depends on how well I use my resources."

It will take some hard work to construct a set of newer, better balanced beliefs, but you can do it — all survivors do, junking the old, irrational belief and adopting a healthier one in its place.

These healthier beliefs all have several things in common. They are truthful, which is to say they are more balanced in the way they describe life. Healthy beliefs do not duck reality, but neither do they drain energy and strength by concentrating on negative aspects of life or by posing impossible demands. They include the positive, hopeful, encouraging possibilities as well as the negative. They are more often tied to immediate, concrete ideas and less to major global pronouncements.

It wouldn't help much, for instance, to replace your old "life-is-hell" belief with a new "life-is-all-roses" belief. The young person who believed that "I am a lousy student; I'll never amount to anything" entertained a huge, defeating evaluation. It helped tremendously to replace that old destructive belief with one that said, "I do have potential as a student, and I will get better if I pay attention to my studies and complete my assignments each day."

Replace your large, depressing, irrational beliefs with healthy, balanced, constructive ones that give concrete instructions on how to act right now. Once you have done that, *practice* your new beliefs throughout the day so that your new healthy way of thinking will become just as ingrained as the old harmful way.

Without realizing it, you may have practiced thinking in negative ways for years. Now, you simply want to start practicing the new way of thinking. Catch yourself when you start dragging up the old thoughts. Remind yourself to "Stop!" and then insert your healthier, better balanced belief.

The Event Contradicts One of My "Big Beliefs"

Big beliefs are religious beliefs or the underpinning philosophy of life. They may be simply larger versions of the life expectations discussed earlier. One very popular book, *When Bad Things Happen to Good People,* by Rabbi Harold Kushner, is devoted exclusively to helping people recover big beliefs in the face of traumatic crisis events.

When a crisis demolishes a big belief you find yourself asking "why" questions. Why would God allow an innocent child to die of leukemia? Why does God permit floods? Why did this happen to me? Why all this suffering and pain?

Often, this is a clue to the fact that the crisis event has challenged some basic view of God, the world, or the universe. You are left with a major set of impossible questions for which there seem no good answers. And any answers attempted will seem weak and shallow or even insulting.

The treatment for recovering big beliefs is very much like that for reordering expectations. The first step in dealing with beliefs that have been contradicted is to recognize that beliefs are cognitive processes that can be controlled and reckoned with. God has not been destroyed; the universe has not altered. It is your *view* of God or the universe that no longer fits with what happened.

The goal is to exchange one set of beliefs — the damaged set — for a new set of beliefs that can account for the crisis event and allow you to face the future.

Ironically, a big belief collapses in a crisis because it was not "big" enough. That is, it was inadequate in some way in the first place. One aspect of growth through a crisis is that when so-called big beliefs are in ruins, more mature beliefs can be built — beliefs that can indeed stand the strain of crisis.

If your big beliefs are in jeopardy during a crisis, make plans to do some philosophical or theological soul-searching in the months ahead. It may have been years since you attended a church or synagogue, or talked to your minister, rabbi, or priest, or thought about reading a Bible. Don't let that get in the way of your search for answers. You need to redefine your beliefs, perhaps reject some of them altogether. But more important, you need to replace them with new ones that both account for what has happened to you and allow you to face the future with hope. This struggle often requires the help of a member of the clergy — or some other sympathetic and understanding person. The newspapers' "Dear Abby" fulfills that function for millions, as shown below:

> Dear Abby: My Sunday school teacher says that God is everywhere. Please put this letter in the paper and maybe he will see it.
> "Dear God: Why did you let my brother die? When he was hit by the car my mother prayed to you to let him live, but you wouldn't. My little brother was only 2 years old and he couldn't have sinned so bad that you had to punish him. Everyone says you are good and can do anything you want to do. You could have saved my little brother, but you let him die. You broke my mother's heart. How can I love you? — Peter"

> Dear Peter: Your question is one that has troubled religious men for thousands of years. One great thinker wrote a book about it. It is called "Job" and is part of the Bible.

It says that the suffering of innocent people is something we cannot understand. But this much is sure: death is not a punishment. It is one of life's mysteries. Speak to your minister, Peter. Communicate with God by praying, and he will help you in your search for wisdom and goodness and help make your mother happy again.

Paradoxically, when all the underpinnings of life are pulled away, such things as faith and hope become supremely important. While other beliefs and assumptions about life may be collapsing all around, many people find that their religious faith carries them through. They discover their faith is more than adequate for survival, and in fact flourishes in times of utmost difficulty — as if they possessed unlimited funds in a bank account they never knew they had.

Often, individuals who have gone through terrible personal catastrophe report that in the midst of their darkest hour they felt God's loving presence as never before. When they realized they could no longer rely on their own strength to master life's circumstances, they found they could depend on God. Newer, deeper, more mature faith can result from the collapse of larger, but wholly inadequate, beliefs.

Take a look at the crisis you are experiencing right now (or perhaps one that occurred some time ago), and ask yourself: Did this crisis involve a challenge to your theological or philosophical beliefs?

Of course, you may not have thought of it in exactly that way till now, but see if the heart of the crisis might have been the fact that you were losing faith — in God, in the future, in the goodness of human beings — a loss of faith that may be discovered now by asking "faith" questions.

Survivors often undergo a theological or philosophical transformation as a result of an intensive search to find answers to questions of faith. They spend time reading Scripture, talking to their pastor, priest, or rabbi, delving into devotional or inspirational books, going to church or temple, attending spiritual workshops — all as part of the process of replacing a damaged big belief.

Some of the world's greatest religious thinkers — Martin Luther, for example — have gone through intense personal crisis that shattered all their carefully reasoned arguments beyond repair. It was out of the pain and despair of rebuilding faith once more that their greatest insights emerged.

Once you understand that it is your *beliefs* that are in jeopardy, not life itself, you then have the issue framed in such a way that you can begin to deal with it. Look closely at your beliefs, seek outside help in developing others that will more accurately guide you through a world changed by your crisis.

The Crisis Event Drags Up Unfinished Business from the Past

Rarely do we neatly conclude the various chapters of our lives before starting new ones. Most of us rush headlong through life toting the baggage of the past, like harried travelers dragging our luggage through crowded terminals after departing trains. We may be scarcely aware of the junk we haul with us, it has become such a part of us.

In a crisis, however, you may become acutely aware of the excess baggage. You feel the weight of it as it contributes to the pain of the crisis.

This is what some psychologists call *unfinished business* — those bits of emotional baggage left over from childhood, adolescence, or young adulthood. Problems, notions, or fears that should have been confronted, dealt with, and laid to rest long ago can suddenly materialize in full force during crisis.

When a young husband's unhappy marriage ends with his wife's leaving him and filing for divorce, for instance, he is understandably devastated by this event. What he may not recognize is that a fair portion of his emotional pain stems from his own lousy self-image, and divorce merely confirms it.

The unfinished business in this instance is the young man's identity development — a process that was never fully completed in late adolescence. Thus, the crisis event (as well as all future crisis events) reinforces a negative self-image.

The simple point in all of this is that much of the pain in what's happening now may be the result of some earlier experience and not exclusively the crisis at hand.

Jill, a young woman who never came to terms with parental authority, began to re-evaluate her life after getting fired from a job that meant a great deal to her. Painful though it was, she looked back over her life and discovered a definite pattern of conflict with authority. Time and time again she had openly shown her distrust and contempt for schoolteachers, professors, police officers, and others in authority roles while growing up. Jill realized she had been walking through life with a chip on her shoulder for anyone in a position of power over her. She came to the unflattering conclusion that her low evaluation in her job stemmed from her hatred of her boss and her hang-up with his supposed misuse of power.

Unfinished business from the past — see if you can discover any that comes to the surface during your own crisis. And remember that now is the time for settling it. Remember, too, the hope in this process.

While the intensity of the present crisis may be due to unfinished business, the hopeful part is that you can now, maybe for the first time in your life, confront these issues from the past and lay them to rest once and for all. You can close the book on some painful business forever and make the necessary changes that will help you later on.

Consider the example above, where Jill's problem with authority got her fired. She soon realized that it had been getting in her way for a long time, though maybe not enough for her to recognize it and deal with it or make a change. She had been misjudging people, prejudging them harshly, moaning about her lot in life and how all these "others" were always getting in the way of her achieving all the success she deserved. Her problem with authority kept her from getting along with people, made her nervous and wary, and much less assertive with superiors. It prevented her from asking for raises when she needed them, from offering good ideas to her boss even when they were asked for, and therefore kept her from advancing in her job as she should have.

But now, as a result of the crisis, the whole issue of authority came to a head. Jill took a good hard look and saw that for much too long her problem had been a serious obstacle, tripping her time and again — at home, at work, in her social life. Her next step was the decision to finish this unfinished business once and for all.

Finishing unfinished business usually involves one of two things: expressing feelings about something that happened long ago (feelings that have been suppressed or repressed) or developing a newer, more realistic understanding of what happened long ago.

We will discuss these in more detail later. For now it is enough to know that unfinished business can be finished by discovering the thread that runs from the past into the current crisis, thereby exaggerating or inflaming it, and then by expressing feelings, or developing a new view of the situation.

The Crisis Shows That I Am Working with the Wrong Program

You wouldn't try to balance your checkbook on a computer using a Pac-Man game program. Nor would you try to find your way around Europe using the toy globe your parents gave you for Christmas when you were in the fifth grade. It simply won't work. You need a new program to balance your checkbook, and a new road map to get around Europe.

As a child, you found ways of coping with life around you that worked very nicely. Those same methods might be barely adequate when you were an adolescent, but if you clung to them as an adult you'd soon find yourself unable to get along at all. You would be attempting to live life as an adult using the infantile methods of a child.

A crisis can radically shift the contours of life so that old ways of coping won't work. You need a new program, a new mental map.

Connie's crisis began the night she had a wreck in her car. No one was hurt — there was very little damage to the car at all. But Connie became distraught when the police asked her to fill out an accident report. Later, when she was taken home, she grew more and more depressed, until she took an overdose of sleeping pills in a weak attempt at suicide.

Connie was a graduate student who had been living from one bad time to the next. She was forever getting herself into scrapes around finances, school grades, and getting her car fixed — each case resulting in a friend, boyfriend, or family member bailing her out.

In therapy following the suicide attempt, she was confronted by her therapist with the fact that she had been using "little girl" ways to get attention and get her needs met for entirely too long. It was time to grow up, develop her own skills for managing adult life (money, automobiles, schooling, relationships), and learn to regard other people as friends and consultants, not as a series of fill-in parents.

If we were to look at her life during the crisis we would say that her life program was one that included faulty instructions on how to get her needs met: Start out on a project by yourself, don't ask for help, but try to do it all alone. Also, never tell anyone you need anything. This would be *giving in* to them (as to parents). But when you eventually get in trouble, scream for help.

Connie's crisis represented a time when her program was revealed as inadequate for adult life. In her case, the crisis following the car accident marked the end — the breakdown — of childish ways of coping, and a brand-new beginning by learning to live life as an adult.

In the rebuilding process, Connie was encouraged to start taking responsibility for herself. For example, she learned how to budget her money, maintain her own car, make and carry out work assignments on her own. It felt strange, and a bit scary at first, taking responsibility for herself — after all, now there was no one else to blame for her failures! But she stuck with it.

Connie began to develop an image of herself as an adult who is responsible for taking care of herself, who consults others for advice but makes decisions and lives with the consequences — *instead* of viewing herself as a kid who couldn't handle responsibility, was dependent upon others to do things for her, and resentful of them when they didn't do it right.

For Connie, the car accident marked the end of childhood and the beginning of a whole new approach to life.

The Crisis Event Overloads the Circuits

Some computers are set up to handle more variables than others; their programs are more complex, and they can store and retrieve more information for processing. The same thing is true of people: depending upon how you were raised and your experiences as you have grown up, your mental program may be capable of handling greater or lesser problems.

A crisis situation arises when the event so overwhelms your mental and emotional programming that the circuits overload. Your program simply cannot handle all that data, all at once.

How does this happen? One way is through an accumulation of stressors from your external environment.

Have a look at the life events listed on pages 120–21.

Research with large numbers of people has shown that each event can be weighted according to its stress value — the death of a spouse is counted as 100 points, marital separation is 65

LIFE EVENTS CHECKLIST*

Life Event	Point Value
1. Death of spouse	100
2. Divorce	73
3. Marital separation	65
4. Jail term	63
5. Death of close family member	63
6. Personal injury or illness	53
7. Marriage	50
8. Fired at work	47
9. Marital reconciliation	45
10. Retirement	45
11. Change in health of family member	44
12. Pregnancy	40
13. Sex difficulties	39
14. Gain of new family member	39
15. Business readjustment	39
16. Change in financial state	38
17. Death of close friend	37
18. Change to different line of work	36
19. Change in number of arguments with spouse	35
20. Mortgage or loan for major purchase (home, etc.)	31
21. Foreclosure of mortgage or loan	30
22. Change in responsibilities at work	29
23. Son or daughter leaving home	29
24. Trouble with in-laws	29
25. Outstanding personal achievement	28
26. Wife begins or stops work	26
27. Begin or end school	26
28. Change in living conditions	25
29. Revision of personal habits	24
30. Trouble with boss	23
31. Change in work hours or conditions	20
32. Change in residence	20
33. Change in schools	20
34. Change in recreation	19

*T. H. Holmes and R. H. Rahe, "The Social Readjustment Rating Scale,"
Journal of Psychosomatic Research 11 (1967): 213–18. Reprinted by permission.

Life Event	Point Value
35. Change in church activities	19
36. Change in social activities	18
37. Mortgage or loan for lesser purchase (car, TV, etc.)	17
38. Change in sleeping habits	16
39. Change in number of family get-togethers	15
40. Change in eating habits	15
41. Vacation	13
42. Christmas	12
43. Minor violations of the law	11

points, going to jail is 63 points, and so on. Each of these events requires a considerable change or adjustment on the part of the individual involved and on family members. The more points you score in a particular year — the more changes in your life — the greater the likelihood of some sort of physical illness: anything from a common cold to a peptic ulcer to cancer. It is as if the body breaks down under all of the stress, telling its owner: "I can't go on like this anymore."

The mechanism by which these life events take their toll is mental. Each event first taxes the brain, putting a strain on the ability to think through problems, decisions, consequences, and plan adjustments, whether due to a divorce, a change in jobs, or the purchase of a house. Each event also requires a change in behavior, but first comes the mental load.

Alex finished college and moved from Ann Arbor to Dallas to take a job as a salesman for an electronics company. Separated from his family, friends, and fiancée, Alex was lonelier than he could have imagined. He told himself that feeling homesick was for kids, that he was old enough to know better. But as the weeks went by, he grew more and more depressed and melancholy.

His new job was far more demanding than he thought it would be when he accepted it; he spent long hours at the of-

122 • THE PHOENIX FACTOR

fice and had little time to get his apartment into shape or to explore his new surroundings. To top it off, the date for his wedding was quickly approaching, and Alex felt he was doing absolutely nothing to get ready for it. He kept telling himself that next week it would get better, but it didn't.

Then came his first road trip as a salesman. Alex made the trip with the sales manager, an ogre who sat back and watched Alex critically, allowing him to make his own mistakes and then pointing them out to him after each sales call. Alex felt as if he were on trial, with the judge peeking over his shoulder and looking for incriminating evidence. By the time the trip was over, Alex had made less than his quota of sales.

Tired, upset, depressed, worried about his job, Alex returned to his still-unfurnished apartment and found an eviction notice taped to his door: he had forgotten to pay the rent before leaving on his sales trip. He went in and threw himself on the bed and cried — all the while thinking, "I'm never going to make it! I can't cope. I'm a failure!"

He did not go in to work on Monday — he'd stayed in bed most of the weekend. When his boss called him Tuesday morning, Alex told him that he was a failure and that he was quitting.

But his boss surprised him by asking him over for dinner that night. Reluctantly, Alex agreed. At dinner Alex's boss told him that he'd seen this happen before, that Alex shouldn't worry too much about it, that he'd adjust in time. Alex doubted it, but kept his doubts to himself. His boss, an older man whose family had grown, asked Alex to spend a few days with him and his wife. "It'll help ease the transition to the South," he said.

That was a breakthrough for Alex. That night the word "transition" kept reverberating through his brain. He had never considered that he had needed an adjustment in moving from school to work, from the East to the South. But the more he thought about it, the more sense it made.

Alex realized that his problem was an overload of stress — the stress of graduating, of starting a new career, of moving to a new place, of planning a new life — it was all too much to take in at one time. It wasn't that he was inadequate; in fact, he had held up pretty well. But the weight of all that change coming so fast was too much for anyone to bear.

The next few weeks were better for Alex, as he found ways to take pressure off himself and give himself time to adjust. When he felt the strain begin to mount, he'd stop and remind himself that he was still in transition, giving himself permission to take it easy. He held off drawing any negative conclusions about his success or failure as a human being, and instead worked at making the necessary changes one at a time.

CHANGING YOUR BELIEFS

After you have discovered what the event means to you and why it has thrown you into crisis (one or more of the seven items described above), the next step is to adjust your beliefs in light of what you have just learned in order to begin facing the future.

This change in beliefs is one of the first places where true growth occurs. For in the process of change, you may develop new attitudes and cast off old conceptions or outdated assumptions about the world, yourself, God, or others. And as a result, you begin to form new beliefs that are healthier and more realistic and that allow greater opportunities for productive life.

Generally, these new beliefs must serve two functions for growth: (1) they must explain or account for what happened, and (2) they must equip you for life in the future.

When we say that the new belief must explain what happened, it means just that. For instance, a man who believed in God and the divine purpose of the universe must somehow find a way to account for the fact that his child has just died.

Where before he had seen God as all powerful, loving, and answering every prayer . . . his belief breaks down when his heartfelt prayer for his son's recovery from leukemia was not answered.

His new belief about God, therefore, must include the fact that his son got sick, he prayed for healing, and the boy died. The new belief — whatever form it takes — must accept that fact and account for it in some way, not deny it.

There are any number of examples of old beliefs breaking down, but the point is that out of the debris of the old belief a newer, more mature, belief must emerge, one that is large enough, comprehensive enough, to include the events of the crisis.

The second function of a new belief is to equip you to face the future. And this must be tested in the basic triad of human life — work, play, and the ability to engage in meaningful relationships with others.

If, as a result of the crisis, your new belief says to you pessimistically that you must never trust another person again, or that the world is not a safe place to live in, the result could be a lifestyle that invites even more problems — a retreat from relationships, paranoia.

The goal of changing your mind, ultimately, is to arrive at a mental attitude that says:

"I am a human being, with strengths and weaknesses, good and bad. I may have thought I could avoid the bad and have all the good, but now I know that I cannot.

"Many of the things I used to believe about myself and about life have undergone a radical change recently. What happened to me is part of my history, part of my life. I want my thoughts about what happened and about my future to be true — not false or distorted. I am going to live in the present, with a view to the future, using the resources that I have available to me. I will capitalize on my strengths, not cling to my weaknesses. I will not deny the past, but rather I will cultivate positive, hopeful images, and encourage and support myself with my own constructive self-talk.

"I will strive for balance in everything I do. If ever I find that my view of the past, or of this crisis event, gets in the way of my living fully in my work, my play or leisure time, or my relationships, then I will stop and determine what the problem is, and I will correct it so that I can go on living as a healthy, productive human being."

For many people, the move to a healthy attitude that can be carried into the future does not come easily. Changing your mind is often hard work, but well worth the effort in the long run. If you are having trouble, finding yourself stuck in one way or another, the suggestions in this chapter and the "Door Openers" presented in the next chapter will help get you moving again.

· EIGHT ·

Door Openers

As we have seen, the threatening events of crisis can overpower the mental machinery temporarily. But as time passes, the mind begins to sort out what happened and why, in an effort to understand and adapt. Dr. Shelley Taylor has studied survivors of severe personal tragedy in order to discover how people adapt mentally to crisis situations. Her research suggests that the mind undertakes three important tasks:

- A search for *meaning* in the events
- An attempt to gain *mastery* over the crisis
- An effort to enhance *self-esteem*

In other words, survivors struggle to understand what has happened and its impact on life, to control the effects of the crisis, and to restore a sense of personal well-being despite the tragedy. None of these tasks is easily accomplished, and it is not unusual for people emerging from crisis to feel as if they are stuck in a gloomy mental closet.

If you find yourself stuck in that same mental closet, consider the following door openers:

1. CHALLENGE YOUR OLD BELIEFS

As we have already pointed out, some crises occur because "old beliefs" collapse under the stress of harsh new realities. Counselors who work in crisis intervention assist their patients in discovering how and why a particular belief or belief system has broken down. You can do this for yourself, however.

Susan had been a member of Ridgeview Church all her adult life — fifteen years under one minister, a man everyone knew as Pastor Tom. When, without warning, the church fired the minister, she became deeply depressed. Pastor Tom was a special friend of Susan's family; he had counseled them through several crises with the children, and she felt very close to him.

Pastor Tom accepted the termination of his ministry gracefully, saying that he, too, thought it was time he meet the challenge of a move to a new congregation. Although there was open argument in the church about the minister's leaving, most church members eventually accepted the decision of the elders.

A year after Pastor Tom had left, the church seemed back on an even keel, and everyone was busy welcoming the new pastor. Everyone except Susan. She could not accept Pastor Tom's absence, and her depression over his leaving had not lessened; if anything it had gotten worse. Susan kept telling her friends in the congregation that her world had collapsed.

Susan did not understand why she couldn't get over the hurt of losing her minister. No one else felt as bad as she did about it — not even Pastor Tom, who was making a new start in a new church. Depressed as she was, Susan felt it impossible to concentrate at work, lost interest in her activities outside the home, grew irritable with her husband, stopped exercising. She still attended church faithfully, but worship was a struggle — all the joy had gone out of it.

One Sunday, as the new pastor was preaching a sermon, Susan, paying only partial attention as she sat rigidly in the pew, heard the words "human beings make mistakes." She didn't think much of it at the time, and the rest of the sermon went by without making much of an impression. But during the next week the words kept coming back to her. She found herself saying time and again: "Human beings make mistakes."

The more she thought about this, the more it made sense. She applied it to her distress over the elders' decision to change ministers. The "mistake" they had made, in her estimation, was dismissing the pastor who meant so much to her. She realized that up to that moment the idea of elders' making errors in judgment had been foreign to her.

She had been raised to believe that the elders were spiritual pillars of the church, led by God to do things according to His will. Thus, elders could do no wrong — they could not make mistakes.

Yet, in her heart Susan believed the elders *had* made a mistake in firing the former pastor, an action wrong for her and wrong for the church. The conflict between this belief and the equally strong belief that elders could not make mistakes had been churning away inside her without her being conscious of it. Her belief about the elders did not square with the fact of the firing. She had become depressed over it without really knowing why.

But she knew now. Susan realized that she needed to change her view of what the elders represented to her, their role in the church, and their human fallibility. These were issues she had never had to deal with before, but as she faced them she came to the conclusion that even if the elders were spiritual leaders, they were still human beings who had made a mistake.

With this new view, Susan wrote each elder a strong letter of disapproval for what they had done; she told them that she felt they had acted improperly and outside the best interests of the congregation, and that although she could not undo their mistake, she hoped they would learn from it, examine their own hearts and see if they did not agree, and use this knowledge to become better leaders in the future than they had been in the last year.

Susan confronted the elders face to face, too — not angrily, but with a spirit of wanting to help them see an error in judgment. In all of this she used her new beliefs about human fallibility to temper her attitude: Elders were human and, like all humans, made mistakes. A belief that was far different from the one she had grown up with as a little girl.

For Susan, the crisis led to a radically different perception of her church and her place in it. It was only when she began grappling with the fact that her beliefs about the elders were the cause of her being stuck in depression that she moved out of the crisis. Once she was able to allow for human failings in the church leaders, then she was able to forgive them and grow into a healthier and more mature attitude.

It may be that simply by getting this far in the book and confronting your own situation, you have already accepted the fact that a belief or expectation about the world no longer "works" for you. Or that some unfinished business is haunting you. The first step toward replacing the defective "old belief" is to confront it head on, to challenge it. You might start by confronting it with sentences like this:

"I can't change what happened, but I can change how I will deal with it, how I will react to it, and how I will interpret it from now on."

"It is my perfectionism (or my need for approval, my poor self-image, or whatever) that is making things so painful for me. If I could get rid of this, maybe I could cope with the rest of it."

Or perhaps, this:

"I must accept the fact that there is a difference between

God as He is, and my view of Him. After all, I am only a human being and can't see God directly. It is my view of God that is breaking down here, not God Himself. What I need is a better understanding of what God is really like."

The idea here is to think a bit more precisely about the particular belief that has broken down, rather than saying to yourself, "Stop feeling sad all the time!" — and then feeling guilty because you feel bad. It is okay to feel sad, or to express negative feelings (as we discussed in Chapter Two). But it is *not* okay to allow yourself to be continually crushed by the weight of an outmoded or inappropriate belief. Challenge it! Change it!

2. GET MORE INFORMATION

Often the growing process gets stuck because you do not have the right information to completely understand the crisis. Once you know which belief or image has broken down — whether it is a view of God, a belief in how the world works, or the basic honesty of humans — see if some new information is required to understand more fully what is going on.

This information can be of two types: new facts about the crisis event itself or new insights into how you might interpret the crisis event.

Many people get mentally stuck in the months and years following a crisis because something about the crisis event itself just doesn't make sense. A divorcee, for example, might not know why her previous marriage failed: Why did her husband leave? Why were the things she had been giving him "never enough"? She might need to talk to her ex-husband or a counselor or a trusted friend to get more information about why the marriage broke up — almost like a "debriefing" exercise.

Examine your thoughts after the crisis. If you find your daily ruminations are filled with questions, it may signal a need for more factual information. The best remedy may be simply to go back to those others who are involved in the event — your ex-spouse, or the physician who diagnosed the illness in your child, or the police officer who was first at the scene of the automobile accident, or the schoolteacher who dismissed your child from class, or the employer who fired you — *anybody* who has facts about what happened — and attempt to fill in the information gap.

Just as you want to have a *reality-based* understanding of the crisis event, you also want to be able to assimilate what has happened, to interpret it to yourself in a meaningful way. You want the "true facts" of the case, but you also want them to make sense for you. The facts alone are worth little if you cannot find a way to make them meaningful to you. If your world view has been shattered by the crisis event, then begin a search for a new view to bring meaning to your life.

This might mean reading books on the subject or talking to others who have gone through what you are going through or asking for advice from others close to you. Bear in mind, however, with all this reading and talking, that you are merely doing research, collecting data. You are under no obligation to believe all you read or hear.

You — not your friends, your parents, your rabbi or pastor, your counselor, or your spouse — are the final judge of what you will believe and what is relevant to your situation. Your job is to research alternatives, uncover new possibilities, find new ways of looking at what has happened that may not have occurred to you before. Get several points of view to compare.

You may not adopt any ideas suggested by your reading or your friends. In fact, you might not even *like* some of the alternatives you find. You don't have to. All you are doing is exploring, gathering information, looking for clues like a detective who is trying to sketch out what happened at the scene of the crime.

The hope is that something someone might say or an idea you might stumble across while reading will strike a nerve inside you and get your own mental process unstuck and moving again.

3. LOOK AT THE FLIP SIDE

This is what good therapists frequently encourage people in crisis to do. A client who comes in fixated on one particular way of looking at the situation is encouraged to try on just the opposite view for a moment.

In the movie *Ordinary People,* a boy whose older brother died in a boating accident is shown talking to his therapist. Up to this point, the boy has been carrying a tremendous load of guilt for his brother's death, as if it was somehow his fault for surviving. The therapist offers this interpretation: The reason you survived and your brother died may be that you were stronger than he was. In other words, the responsibility for the death rests with the one who died. This idea was exactly the opposite of what the boy had been thinking before.

Try looking at your situation in just the opposite way, and see if you get any new ideas or new insights into the crisis event that you might have overlooked.

4. LOOK FOR THE OPPORTUNITY

Earlier in this book, we pointed out that the Chinese symbol for crisis is danger *and* opportunity combined. Up to this point in the crisis you may have been concentrating only on the danger aspects: the pain, the trauma, the threat, the loss of everything you hold dear. That is natural, of course. But right now, for a few moments, think of the *opportunity* part of it.

This may not come easily, and perhaps not without guilt. But no one can see your thoughts, so put a check on the guilt for the time being and explore any possibilities for positive growth.

Helen suspected that her husband had been having an affair for several months. When he finally admitted it and told her that he was moving out and taking an apartment across town, she took it calmly and let him go. In the days that followed, however, she became angrier and angrier.

One morning she got into her car and drove to the new apartment, where she simply walked in without knocking on the door, surprising her husband and his lover in the kitchen. Helen had worked herself up into such a rage that the moment she saw them together she flew into the woman, attacking her with her fists. Her husband called the police; it was all he could do to hold them apart from one another until the police arrived.

Helen returned home after the incident scared, humiliated, and hurt. Her feelings had not improved at all by the time the divorce proceedings began. She remained bitter and resentful, and she was embarrassed that she was losing her husband and angry that he found this other woman attractive. For many weeks after the divorce became final, she told herself she desperately wanted him back, and sometimes planned strategies she might use to get him back.

But as time went on, she noticed a strange thing: She discovered that since he had left she felt much freer than she had before, more independent. Life seemed more exciting than it had in a very long time. She surprised herself by admitting to a friend that she was actually enjoying the fact that she was free again. Life was quieter around the house since her husband was not there to criticize her and pick at her. She had more time for friends and projects of her own.

Helen found, much to her surprise, that solitude agreed with her. She welcomed being alone and relished the fact that she had no one else to be responsible for. Her previously dull existence suddenly took a whole new direction when she enrolled at the university to begin working toward a new career. And though she had never thought much about working before — her husband did not approve of women having "careers" — she discovered she had a flair for accounting and decided to get her degree and become a CPA.

Helen discovered the enormous opportunity hidden in the hellish circumstances of her husband's affair and their ensuing divorce. She could have nursed the negative feelings and remained forever hurt and bitter, but she embraced the opportunity side of the crisis and it changed her life.

The fact is that most events in life bring with them both gains and losses. This is true even in very bad situations — the death of a spouse, for example. While not denying the awful pain in the loss of a loved one, the fact is that many new doors are opened: it may be the freedom to go back to school, to pursue a new career, to travel.

Getting fired from one job, while depressing and financially frustrating, actually offers the opportunity to make a clean break to another kind of work, to explore other talents, to create a new and different kind of life altogether. Many people who have lost their jobs point to the event later as a "turning point" (interestingly, the Latin definition of *crisis*) that changed their lives for the better.

Sadly, however, many people never allow themselves to think about the positive side of the crisis because they think it shows disrespect for what happened; they feel guilty benefiting from tragedy, so to speak. But this is a somewhat distorted view of the situation, since it is only a partial view. A more wholistic view recognizes that there are two separate truths in operation here.

One truth says that yes, something has changed — someone died, someone left, someone had an affair, someone lost a limb, someone became ill, and so on. The other truth says that as a result of this traumatic change, some opportunities are present that were not present before. Both truths are opposite sides of the same coin, and both should be recognized.

5. REASSESS PERSONAL VALUES

Recovery and growth are impossible following many crises without a change in personal values. It may well be that your view of the purpose of life, your sense of what is most important, or your arrangement of your priorities, is what got you into trouble in the first place. Think of the husband whose commitment to financial gain at all cost, with continued neglect of spouse and children, leads to a failed marriage that ends in divorce. Or the entrepreneur whose unwillingness to share power forces partners to desert him in order to survive and grow themselves.

Look at your own crisis. If the unfolding events have exposed bankrupt values, or twisted priorities, then ask yourself a few questions:

• If an observer had seen me before this crisis, what might he have concluded about my values and priorities?

• What is most important to me now?

• If I treat this crisis as a milestone, what changes do I want to make in attitudes, beliefs, and values as I face the future?

Write your answers down on paper. Talk to others whose lives are dedicated to wrestling with issues of values and priorities — your pastor, rabbi, priest. Follow these conversations with reading to further your pilgrimage. Instead of looking for a quick overhaul, think of yourself as being on a path to rediscover what is truly important in life. Seriously examining your values may be all you need to open the door.

6. ADMIT GUILT

If you were wrong, or responsible for some aspect of the crisis, you may be plagued by feelings of guilt, without knowing what to do about them.

Suppose you are stuck in a swamp of angry feelings toward your boss for your having been passed over for a promotion or for having been fired. Till now you may have concentrated on how wrong your boss was and how badly he treated you.

But, somewhere in your heart, you know that you're seeing only part of the picture. Gnawing away at your conscience is the idea that maybe you fouled up your own promotion; maybe you actually deserved to get fired. Maybe it was your fault. You think back on things you should have done and failed to do, things you could have said that might have made a difference. Thoughts such as these build and become another form of punishment, often hurting more than the original loss.

Most people have thoughts of this kind but have no idea where to go from there. Having stumbled onto the notion that they are partly responsible for their own misfortune, they get bogged down there and flounder, unable to proceed.

Accepting responsibility for your part in the crisis is the first step in working through guilt. Alcoholics Anonymous, one of the world's largest and most successful self-help groups, includes this step in their program, suggesting that their members take a "moral inventory" and share it with another person. Later in the program, members must make amends in whatever way they can for the problems they've caused while drinking.

If you are stuck, you might consider the need to begin taking responsibility for the part you yourself may have played in the present crisis.

7. ALLOW FORGIVENESS

Any admission of guilt must also leave open the possibility of forgiveness.

When we speak of forgiveness, unfortunately the phrase "forgive and forget" comes to mind. Many people, perhaps because of this aphorism, believe that to forgive is to simply forget that the unhappy event ever happened.

The truth is you *cannot* forget; you will never forget. You will never forget the fact that your child was sexually molested, that your husband had an affair, or that you have suffered terribly in one way or another through the crisis.

You *can*, however, keep the event from gaining a strangle hold on you for the rest of your life. You can keep it from poisoning your emotional life through hate, jealousy, bitterness, or any of the other negative, debilitating emotions.

And forgiveness may be the only way to achieve this. Granting forgiveness, if you are the person wronged, frees you from the awful tyranny of the darker forces of human nature. You forgive as much for yourself as for the person who has harmed you or caused you pain.

To forgive means to pardon someone, to let go of resentment. Forgiveness says, "I accept the fact of what happened, I understand why it happened, and I will no longer allow it to interfere with my life or my relationship with you."

The concept of forgiveness is central in the Judeo-Christian religious tradition. The teachings of the prophets and of Jesus, who even forgave those who crucified him, can offer a model for responding to a friend, a spouse, a neighbor, an employer, a stranger, or anyone else who might be responsible in some way for your crisis.

Many people are not aware of the role of forgiveness within their own religious tradition. Many Christians, for instance, forget that the same order of worship that has a "confession of sin" also includes an "assurance of pardon." In the Christian tradition, accepting God's forgiveness is just as important as confessing the sin.

If you are stuck on the crisis event, unable to move forward and begin the healing, growing process, it might be that forgiveness can free you. You might start by merely asking yourself: "If I were to forgive _____ for what happened, what would that do to my future?" It might do a great deal.

8. ACCEPT THE UNKNOWN

The ultimate knowledge and explanation of life rests with God, and not with your own finite brain. You may never completely understand why certain people die, why pain occurs, why things happen the way they do.

But once you can accept the fact that you cannot know everything, you free yourself from a lot of agonizing over questions that have no answers in this life. Keep working to find answers, but don't lose sight of your own human limitations in the process.

9. CONSIDER PRAYER

The World War I saying that there are "no atheists in foxholes" is often used as a rather cynical commentary on the human condition. Still, people do become aware of their own spiritual needs during times of crisis, and many who have never prayed suddenly call out to God for help. The annals of religious literature are filled with accounts of conversion during crisis that follow this pattern.

Theologians remind us that prayer is more than a self-centered "SOS" message. In most religious traditions prayer is only one aspect of a continuing relationship with God. Crisis often brings with it the awareness of our own mortality, our inability to control our own destiny, our need for help from a higher power, all of which puts us in touch with the spiritual dimension of our lives.

Prayer may begin by simply unloading problems and worries, asking for help and guidance, seeking reassurance. Start any way you wish, and then listen for unexpected answers: the wise advice of a friend or the counsel of a religious leader, the fortuitous unfolding of events, a sudden insight that brings comfort or a new direction, restored confidence in the future.

10. SHARE THE RESPONSIBILITY

People sometimes get stuck in the aftermath of a crisis when they attempt to saddle one person with the entire blame.

While this is a natural enough reaction, it is usually wrong. Life is complex — the reasons why things happen as they do are never simple. There are usually no single causes, but rather multiple causes, even in the most straightforward events.

In an automobile accident, for instance, a teenager is killed by a drunken driver. To be sure, the drunk whose pickup crossed the median and plowed head-on into a carload of girls caused the accident. But what about the argument the young girl had with her parents over joyriding with those other kids? Or the father who says, "I should never have given in and let her go?" What about the mother who blames herself for not being more strict in her daughter's choice of friends? What about the surviving friend who says to herself, "If only I had insisted we go to the movie like I wanted to"?

The list goes on and on. In the heat of crisis it is normal to want to assign blame — to take responsibility for what happened or to try to fault someone else. The fact is, however, that in almost any crisis, such as the accident just mentioned, there are *multiple* causes.

Multiple causes mean multiple responsibilities. It won't help to take on more than your share of the responsibility, nor to load blame unfairly on anyone else.

◆ ◆ ◆

All of the "door openers" discussed so far show how to deal with what happened in the past. The following suggestions show how you can begin looking to the future with hope.

11. USE "GROWTH" WORDS

Some survivors think of crisis as growing pains. Others talk about a crisis tempering their lives (like steel), or seasoning them (like good food), so that even though the event may be painful when it happens, they become stronger or better as a result. Using "growth" words means adopting growth-oriented concepts to help describe the present and carry you into the future.

The words you use to describe your experience really do make a difference in how you move through the crisis. Often, by talking about your crisis experience in an appropriate way, you begin to think about it in a new and healthier light. Words do more than simply "describe" what you are thinking or feeling; they can also help *shape* your thoughts and emotions.

If you are stuck and want to plow through the morass, try using words that describe the growth potential of the crisis — the *learning* and *developing* aspect of the experience.

Early in the crisis, you probably used words like these to describe how you felt:

LOST	HURT	ALONE
SHOCKED	ANGRY	DEVASTATED
HOPELESS	BITTER	SAD

Your thoughts (and speech) probably contained many sentences like: "I can't go on!" "I've had it!" "I'm terribly afraid." "I'll never make it."

Describing the crisis in this way — which is certainly appropriate early in the crisis — will ultimately lead to a dead end unless you take steps to change it.

As you move through the crisis allow your language to reflect the opportunity aspect of the crisis: the opportunity to *learn* new skills, to *broaden* your perspective on life, to *deepen* your appreciation of others around you, to *discover* hidden strengths.

Look at these words for a moment:

LEARN	DEVELOP
BROADEN	DEEPEN
DISCOVER	GAIN

These words, and others like them, characterize different aspects of growth. Use them in sentences like the following:

"I am learning to take care of myself."

"I am discovering strengths I never dreamed I had."

"I am finding out that I can cope with anxiety and sadness and with not knowing exactly what will happen next."

"I am developing new ways of relating to others."

"I am broadening my awareness of life around me."

"I am becoming more thankful."

"I am gaining a greater appreciation of life."

"I am deepening my understanding of love."

Expressing the growth side of a crisis is not the same as "sugar coating" the experience — it's a way of opening the door by matching your vocabulary to the reality of psychological growth.

12. EXERT SOME CONTROL

Even though some very important parts of your situation may be well out of your control, it helps to be able to exert control over those aspects of your situation that can be influenced.

Studies of patients with life-threatening illnesses show that rather than fretting about the things that are now beyond their direct control, survivors learn to shift their energies to things that they can do something about — actively participating in their medical treatment, for example.

This is a recognized technique of stress management. One well-known psychologist describes driving to his office through horrendous early morning traffic jams. His way of handling the stress of the commute is to exert control in some way. Even though he cannot direct the flow of traffic, he *can* control his own car. So, as he moves through bumper-to-bumper traffic, six lanes wide, he periodically slows his speed at ramps and motions for another driver to go in front of him. In that small way, for a moment or two, he controls the traffic. This sense of control over his situation, even though it is limited, combats the frustration and anger that often result from traffic jams.

Similarly, a study of prisoners of war found that many maintained their sanity by the way they arranged their meager personal belongings in their cells. For example, when enemy interrogators came in, the POWs would stand up and offer a chair, directing their captors to a particular section of the room. While their lives were controlled by the keepers of the prisons, the POWs made good use of even the smallest opportunities to exert control — deciding where their interrogators sat — thus gaining a sense of mastery of the situation.

You can do the same sort of thing when emerging from the ashes of your own crisis. Look for some part of your life, or your environment, that you can control — and exert some control over it.

13. DO SOME GOOD, RIGHT SOME WRONG

This is akin to forgiveness, and may serve to bring both mastery and increased self-esteem to your recovery. Although you may not be able to undo the hurt and wrong brought about by the crisis, you may be able to channel some of your own energy into constructive action so others need not suffer in the same way you did. This might mean working for a worthy cause related to your own crisis, righting a wrong, or in some way making a commitment to help someone else.

It is not uncommon among those who have successfully resolved crises to find the following: victims of rape who later serve as counselors in rape crisis clinics, or parents of children stricken with leukemia who work in organizations to help other families similarly afflicted. Candy Lightner, for example, founded Mothers Against Drunk Driving (MADD) after her own child was killed by a drunk driver. Lois Gibbs became leader of the Love Canal protests after her own children became ill from the chemical wastes buried in their neighborhood.

While these activities relate more directly to the behavioral changes to be discussed in the next chapter, the *decision* to transform one's inner pain into activity that may help others who are undergoing similar crisis situations can be a critical door opener in the mental mastery of the crisis. This sort of commitment is often the first step toward helping move into the future in a constructive way.

14. PRACTICE POSITIVE SELF-TALK

One of the more powerful psychotherapy tools involves using positive self-talk: substituting constructive thoughts for destructive ones on a regular basis thoughout the day. Self-talk is nothing more than the statements you "tell" yourself; it's the inner dialogue you carry on with yourself all the time.

During a crisis, when life is generally bad, your self-talk is likely to reflect all the negative things you're thinking and feeling.

Therapists have learned, however, that one very good way to change negative feelings and destructive behavior is to change the thoughts behind them. How you think about something directly affects how you act and feel. By substituting positive thoughts and images for negative ones and making a practice of telling them to yourself regularly, you will begin thinking and acting in healthier and more constructive ways.

Positive self-talk begins with any phrase or statement that helps capture your resolve to overcome the crisis. It might grow from a good experience with one of the door openers presented earlier in this chapter. Perhaps your soul searching and conversations with friends have resulted in a belief that "I will survive" or "God cares about me; He will see me through" or "I'm a smart person, I can learn to adapt" — or some other hopeful view. When you find a phrase or statement that offers hope, make a point to practice repeating it regularly throughout the day.

Practice is important because it takes repetition to counter negative thoughts and to introduce positive alternatives into our daily mental lives. Some people go through the day evaluating their performance critically, telling themselves, "That was sure a stupid thing I did. I never do anything right!" Overcoming the negative tendencies, however, takes practice — the same kind of practice needed to develop any new skill, from playing the piano to swinging a golf club. By *practicing* positive self-talk you gradually build a habit of thinking positively.

Counselors have found that people who suffer intense anxiety when confronted with new social situations are often *hurting themselves* by repeating over and over damaging statements like, "I know I'll make a fool of myself" or "I'm going to be embarrassed, I know it." Their negative self-talk makes for a self-fulfilling prophecy; they actually confirm their own worst fears.

The trick with positive self-talk is to catch yourself repeating something negative and immediately say to yourself, "Stop that!" Then back up and remind yourself of something positive about your situation, or repeat the positive phrase or statement that helps you create a more hopeful mental atmosphere.

Positive "self-talk" is especially helpful when you are tempted to start feeling sorry for yourself or lamenting your fate. At times like these, when it's very difficult to think positively, sit down and make a list of statements that are true and also offer hope, and then keep that list before you throughout the day.

Think of phrases that enhance your self-esteem, such as: "I am learning to take better care of myself" or "I've been through a tremendous ordeal, but I am coping better every day." Or phrases that mobilize your strengths, like, "I may have been fired, but I know I have good skills and I'm going to keep trying" or "The worst is behind me now; I know I'm going to make it."

As you move out of the crisis, determined to face the future yet find yourself stuck periodically, have a look at what you're saying to yourself. It may be that you are slipping back into negative self-talk without realizing it. Making a determined effort to think in more hopeful terms — literally repeating positive statements to yourself throughout the day — can change your situation dramatically.

15. USE POSITIVE IMAGERY

To truly maximize the possibility of moving ahead with your new way of looking at yourself and the world, draw on the strengths of both hemispheres of the brain. Just as your positive self-talk makes use of the left side of your brain (your language center), positive mental pictures or images make use of the right (your image center).

The value of positive images is well known in sports. Many coaches train their athletes to picture in their minds the perfect golf stroke or tennis swing or baseball pitch. A tennis player, for example, imagines herself on the court, feeling healthy, ready, energetic, watching the ball, anticipating its approach, making the right moves to get into position to return it, bringing the racket back in plenty of time to begin the stroke, hitting the ball squarely, and sending it back over the net perfectly.

This positive imagery shows her succeeding in what she wants to do. This works not only for athletes but for everyone else as well. The idea is to picture yourself succeeding in living out your new beliefs, making new plans, and coping with life ahead.

We are not talking about dreaming up some fairy tale fantasy and trying to sell yourself on it. Rather, the idea is to build on any newfound sense of meaning following the crisis, or on your resolve to regain control of your life, or on steps you have taken to rebuild your self-esteem. Picture yourself surviving, getting along, living in the future the way you would like to. Let yourself have a fantasy or image of what you would like your life to be in the future. Picture yourself living in this changed situation — maybe it's living in a different town or a different house, having a new job, making new friends. Whatever you will need to make it in your new world, include it in your mental picture.

It might help to look to a friend you admire, or someone who has survived what you are now going through. What is she doing that appeals to you? What characteristics of his life stand out to you? What makes this person a good model for you? Find out what he is doing, the characteristics of his life that appeal to you, and add these positive attributes to your mental image of the future. You aren't trying to "be" that other person, but feel free to adopt any features you will need in order to succeed.

If you cannot *imagine* the possibility of surviving, how can you expect to do it? If you have difficulty seeing yourself involved in a meaningful new life in the future, it will be even more difficult for you to achieve it. You must be able to picture a hopeful future before you can begin making it a reality. Picturing yourself succeeding at the thing you're setting out to achieve can be more than half the battle! Use the door openers from this chapter to begin forming a mental picture of how you would like your life to be in the future.

◆   ◆   ◆

Everything we have described in this chapter involves the cognitive or mental aspects of growth. We have shown how getting into a crisis is in many respects a mental phenomenon, and therefore getting out of it involves a mental process, too. Survivors find that mastering the crisis mentally is a necessary step toward growth. The mental mastery we have described in this chapter is what makes managing feelings, taking care of your body, and making behavioral adjustments really work.

Cognitive mastery of the crisis means understanding what happened and understanding how the crisis event conflicts with your expectations for life; it means developing a view of life that allows you to think of yourself living in the future in a productive and satisfying way.

Total mental mastery of a crisis rarely happens overnight. It takes time. A new thought that adds to your understanding of what happened can occur to you many months or even years later — a paragraph in a book, a sermon, a movie, or a conversation with a friend may spark new awareness or insight into the nature of the crisis. Your cognitive mastery is thereby helped along a bit, your understanding is refined.

Thus, the mastery process goes on and on. While we have

listed numerous door openers in this chapter, you may find some useful now and others more helpful in the future. Some doors are ready to be opened now, others may need to wait until later. Do what you can now; do what you are ready to do. It may also be helpful to come back and review this chapter at a later date.

The suggestions presented in this chapter will help you begin thinking in more constructive ways if you have become "stuck" mentally or fixated on one aspect of the crisis. Once you have made the decision to start living again and are ready to face the future, you are ready to begin adjusting your behavior to fit your new world, which is the subject of the next chapter.

NINE

Adjusting Your Behavior

DEEP-SEA DIVERS often descend into ocean depths where the atmospheric pressure is many times greater than that normally experienced on dry land. The deeper they dive, the greater the pressure. Their bodies adjust to the increased pressure as they go down and down into the depths.

When it is time to come up, however, the diver must be wary; his long swim back to the surface must be accomplished very carefully. If he ascends too quickly he will get the bends — an excruciatingly painful, potentially fatal, condition caused by too rapid decompression. Therefore, he must swim up slowly, with special stops along the way to allow his body to readjust to lower pressure.

This deep-sea–diver analogy has a special application for a person working through a crisis. You, like a diver, have left your normal environment; due to the crisis, you are now living in a drastically changed world.

Life will never be exactly the same for you, now that you have . . . lost your job, lost a loved one, gone through the ordeal of surgery, endured the strain of a move from your hometown, or whatever has caused your crisis. Not only will your life be different in certain physical respects — new surroundings, the absence of a partner, diminished abilities, a change in daily routine — from now on your life will be different in a psychological sense as well.

Having experienced powerful feelings, having been terrorized by the thoughts and images that have been with you in the past weeks and months, having endured the nightmares, you are truly a changed person. You hold the memory of what you have been through, and life can never be exactly the same as it was before.

This is neither bad nor good — it's simply the way things are. Like the diver, you are living life in a different "atmosphere" than before the crisis; emerging from the upset and confusion means adjusting to a new environment, a world radically changed by the events of the crisis. And like the deep-sea diver, adjusting involves stopping along the way to allow yourself time to get used to the new atmosphere. After the death of a spouse, you can't develop a new social life overnight, for instance; nor can you instantly learn to use an artificial limb.

You begin with a few changes in behavior — perhaps the ones forced on you by the crisis — and live with these for a while until you get used to them. Then you try a few more changes. Eventually, you find yourself living in a radically changed world.

We want this chapter to serve as a guide for changing your behavior after a crisis, but don't try to do it all at once. Change takes time. It might be that the information in this chapter seems more scary than helpful. "How can I ever hope to do all this?" you may wonder. One step at a time is the answer — and with plenty of rest stops along the way.

Think of changes in how you act or behave — on the job, toward family and friends, as you move through the day — as the bottom line of growing through any crisis.

How you adjust your actions — work, play, relationships, daily routine, and care of your body — in response to the trauma is ultimately the most important aspect of growing through the crisis. Behavioral change is the true measure of how successful you are in resolving the crisis. Eventually, you will have to ask yourself: Can I return to the business of living? Am I equipped to face the future?

Talking about changing behavior threatens most people a little. We hate to give up favorite bad habits. We get depressed if we can't follow through on good intentions. Change is hard, frightening.

But remember the opportunity present in crisis. It's the dark cloud's silver lining: when everything has been rearranged by crisis, it's easier to make lasting changes than when life is stable, with patterns fixed.

FIRST THINGS FIRST

• Doris, fired from her job, suddenly finds herself without income. How will she handle the bills for the next month or so?

• John lost his wife of fifteen years to a stroke. A funeral must be planned and the family contacted.

• Allen moved from a small college in the Midwest to a large university in the East to begin graduate school. He must find an apartment, register for classes, find reliable transportation, begin making new friends.

• Bobbi was raped. She must contact the police, undergo a physical exam, decide whether to return to her apartment, deal with friends who will want to know what happened.

For each of these people, as for anyone experiencing a crisis, the first step in adjusting behavior is to *take care of first things first*. Do those things absolutely necessary to "cover your bases," and let the rest wait until later. (See Chapter Three for a refresher on making immediate decisions.)

But as time goes on and the immediacy of the crisis event recedes, just making-do is hardly a satisfactory way to live. We can start by looking closely at the kinds of changes you may have to make to live in the "new world" created by the crisis. Here, a list can be helpful in deciding where to start.

TAKE INVENTORY

An inventory is simply a list of items on hand. All sorts of businesses use them: A grocer's inventory tells him which items to restock. Builders make inventories before beginning construction; they need to know what materials they have to work with. In beginning to take the first critical steps toward growth, start by looking at what you have to work with — in particular, what your strengths and weaknesses are — as you start rebuilding your life.

A personal inventory begins with the recognition that all areas of your life have been affected by the crisis. In one way or another the crisis has touched everything about you.

If you look closely at each major area of your life — work, relationships, physical health, leisure — and take note of how you are functioning in that area right now, you can see areas of strength as well as areas of weakness.

For example, Doris may have been fired, but she has a loving relationship with her husband. John may have lost his wife, but he has a strong network of caring friends. Allen may be confused and disoriented by his academic move, but he enjoys his studies.

Your situation will be no different. Even though they may seem hidden at times, there will be areas of strength that can be used to offset the weaknesses. Your strengths will be your foundation, the resources to mobilize in moving into the future. Weaknesses are the areas in which you need to begin making gradual adjustments.

Many people have written about ways to categorize life activities. Sigmund Freud thought that a healthy, productive life involved meaningful work, positive loving relationships, and the ability to play. This provides a good start: work, relationships, leisure.

However, in keeping with more recent research on the connection between physical and mental health, it is important to consider the activities involved in taking care of the body, too. So, adding that to the list, we have an inventory made up of four parts: work, relationships, physical health, and leisure.

Work

This section can be divided into two categories: (1) job- and career-related concerns and (2) the daily chores of maintaining life. To help you start off in the right direction in evaluating the elements of these two basic categories, the next few pages will present two questionnaires (one for each of the categories) and a discussion of each, with examples of how to make the questions work for you. Spend a few minutes looking at them, and then fill them out. On the blank line before each item, rate yourself: " + " if you feel you are doing all right or very well in that area or " − " if you feel things could be better if some changes could be made.

Note that a mark of " + " means that the item is under control and you are happy with it the way it is; a " + " identifies an area of strength. Weaknesses are the areas that need your attention in the months ahead as you learn to live in a world changed by the crisis.

After rating each category, jot something down in the column at the right. Ask yourself specifically, "What is going well in this area?" or "What needs changing?"

1. Job/Career. Many crisis events can affect your career in some way — you may be required to get a new job, learn how to work differently, face the difficulty of returning to the job after an absence. Unemployment is the most obvious example where behavioral adjustments center on work. The most pressing adjustment in unemployment will be to get a new job. Another example might be if you became disabled and were unable to return to the work you used to do.

In either case, and for many other crises, the growing edge for you would be to find different and more satisfying work. And, as so often happens, you could well discover that you have talents and abilities you have never explored before, maybe some you never even knew you possessed.

Another important aspect to consider when taking an inventory of your career-related environment is money. Lose a job and you lose income; the two are eternally bound together. A crisis that affects the job front will generally affect the pocketbook in some way as well — usually in a most dramatic way. So, in beginning adjustment to a post-crisis environment, you will want to carefully examine the financial aspect of work.

1. Job/Career

Specific Category	How is this a strength? or What needs changing?
— Cash flow for the next three months	
Do I have enough money coming in to take care of expenses for the next three months?	
— A satisfying job	
Do I have a job? Do I like the job I have? Will I need to find a new job?	

Will I need new skills or training to
  get a new job?
Do I need to go back to school to get
  a degree or credential?

— Longer-term financial needs

  Do I need to change my will,
    investments, or mortgage?
  Develop a new financial plan for the
    next several years?

— Other

  Any other concerns about my job or
    career?

Here's an example of how the above section of the inventory
might be filled out:

When Gladys was widowed at the age of forty-four and left
with the care of a ten-year-old boy and twin eight-year-old
girls, her rating on the job/career category looked like this:

1. A "+" under Cash Flow, since the insurance company
had delivered a check that would take care of things for ap-
proximately six months. That took care of a very big concern
for her. Also, an attorney friend had already offered to help
her review her entire financial picture after things settled down
a bit.

2. A "–" under Satisfying Job, with her comments to the
right:

> "I don't have a job now, since my volunteer work has
> been the only thing I have done outside the home until
> Jim died."

> "I have no skills, don't know what I would like to do,
> and don't know if I could get a job anyway."

> "I will probably need to go back to school, but don't
> know how much that would cost."

3. A " – " under Other:

"I don't know what to do with the kids after school."
Gladys had always been there to greet her children when
they came home from school, though she foresaw that
she would likely be working full time and would therefore have to make different arrangements.

This was how Gladys filled out her inventory. Yours,
of course, will look very different, depending on your circumstances.

2. Maintenance. The second category of work, maintenance,
includes a whole range of mundane activities — everything
from writing checks, paying bills on time, buying groceries,
cooking meals and doing dishes, to cleaning the bathroom
regularly. Also included under the maintenance section of the
inventory are shelter and transportation.

After a crisis, some people cannot physically take care of
their own maintenance. For instance, a man who injured his
back in an accident at work was not able to dress himself for
some time. In addition to helping in this task, his wife had to
find some way to get the lawn mowed, the car serviced,
and the garbage taken out, all of which had been his responsibilities.

Often, a crisis will create new challenges in the regular routine of life. A family whose breadwinner is ill or out of work
may not have enough money to repair the car, which creates
problems in the area of transportation: How can you get
around to find a job if you don't have a car? How can you get
your car repaired if you don't have a job?

So think about the items on the following questionnaire and
fill it out as you did the one on job/career: " + " for items of
strength and " – " for areas where changes need to be made.
Then spend a few minutes considering any changes that could
be made to make a particular item better.

2. Maintenance

Specific Category	Strengths? or Changes needed?

— Household chores

Are they being taken care of now in an
acceptable way?
Do I need help with them?
Do I need to learn some new skills to do
them?
Do I need to talk to my spouse/partner
about them and negotiate a change?

— Transportation

Do I have adequate transportation?
Is my car in good repair?
Do I need to work out a better system of
transportation or find better ways to take
care of the transportation I have?
Do I need a new(er) car?

— Time management

Do I have enough time to take care of the
chores I have?
Do I have enough time and energy for
work, family, and my own interests?
Am I using the time I have most
effectively?

— Shelter

Is my current housing adequate?
Do I need to find a new place to live?
Are there any repairs I need to make?
Do I need new furnishings?

— Other

Any other concerns about my daily living?

Tom and Josie, whose crisis involved marital difficulties that surfaced after the birth of their third child, filled out the maintenance category of the inventory together:

1. Household Chores were a definite minus for Josie. Tom had done nothing to contribute in this area for some time. His view was that if he worked hard at the office, bringing in good money, then he shouldn't have to lift a finger around the house. While this approach worked in the early years of their marriage, it had completely broken down with increased family size. Josie was physically exhausted and worried about having her identity tied up exclusively in housework. She wanted to get out of the house more. Josie wrote:

> "Find a way to get Tom to help more, or hire someone to take care of the house so I can do other things. This is going to be difficult!"

2. Transportation was a plus for them. Josie had never had to even think about the car because Tom took care of keeping the automobile in tiptop shape at all times. Tom was a little less than enthusiastic about this since he felt Josie could at least try to remember to get the oil changed from time to time so that he wouldn't always have to do it. Still, they rated the item a plus because no real changes were necessary for the present.

3. Josie rated Time Management a minus. She clearly felt that there was never enough time to do all the things she wanted to do in a day. Her comments were:

> "We're saying 'Yes' to too many activities. It's got to stop."

> Tom added: "Maybe we should get better organized."

4. Both rated Shelter as a plus. Their house was comfortable and adequate for their needs. They had been able to add a room for the new baby, and both were grateful for a good place to live.

5. Under Other, Josie put a minus and wrote:

> "The yard is always a mess. I wish there was a way we

could agree whose job it was to take care of the lawn and garden. Tom seems to expect me to do everything but mow and rake."

Relationships

Perhaps the most obvious area of behavioral change following a crisis is the area of personal relationships. Many crises directly involve another person — divorce, conflicts at work, rape, or physical assault. However, whether the crisis is a direct result of a problem with another person or stems from other causes, such as illness or injury, every crisis will have some effect on the people close to you: family, friends, employers, co-workers, people you come into contact with after the crisis.

A crisis will often expose weaknesses in relationships. For example, a couple who had never expressed their deeper feelings to one another may find it difficult to communicate in the aftermath of a traumatic event. An unwanted move, disablement, unemployment, or any other crisis situation will be much harder to deal with because the couple is not skilled in talking about their feelings, sharing burdens, and developing solutions together.

Below are some typical adjustments that arise in relationships.

Spouse/Partner. If you are just widowed or divorced, the adjustment is to learn to live alone. Later it might involve finding a new partner. In other cases, the adjustments could be in how you relate to your spouse or partner. Following some marital crises drastic changes are made in communication, division of household chores, making love, spending time together.

Family. A family is a social system that has certain ways of operating. Every family develops its own way of dealing with anger, expressing affection, making decisions, and handling daily maintenance. When a crisis strikes, most of the family system's operating methods are suddenly changed. As with virtually any system, a change in one part of the system will produce changes in other parts via the ripple effect.

In some instances adjustments will be quite obvious; maybe something as simple as the fact that the family needs to spend more time talking and listening to one another. Other adjustments may require some concentrated thought or effort to discover: the family's normal way of handling conflict is causing emotional problems for one of its members, and a new way of dealing with anger must be found.

The growth opportunity here is that a family can learn new and better ways of relating to one another through a crisis — changes that would never have come about had the crisis not occurred.

Friendships. It is not uncommon for friendships to shift radically following a crisis. You might be cut off from friends, or lose one, or face circumstances that make it difficult to relate to your friends in the way you did before the crisis. The objective now is to find out what adjustments must be made in order for friendships to be resumed, repaired, or developed anew.

Social Groups. Beyond your immediate circle of family and friends, you are related to other groups: clubs, professional organizations, religious organizations, civic groups. You may have a very remote relationship with any or all of these groups, but in a sense they are there for you if you need them. You may, for example, find yourself more involved with your local church or temple as a result of the crisis, or involved with a self-help group like Alcoholics Anonymous or Al-Anon. Your main concern now is to examine your relationships with the various social groups in your network and find out if these relationships are all you wish them to be.

These, then, are the four areas of concern under the relationship section of your inventory. Examine each area on the following questionnaire and fill it out, using "+" for areas of strength and "−" where definite changes must be made.

Relationships

Specific Category	Strength? or Changes needed?

— Spouse/Partner

    Am I adjusting to the loss of a partner?
    Do I need to find ways to meet new people
       who might be potential partners?
    Or, do I need to make certain changes in
       the way I relate to my partner:
          Conflict resolution?
          Decision making?
          Communication?
          Negotiation skills?
          Assertiveness?

— Family

    Do I need to spend more time with family
       members?
    How is communication right now?
    Discipline?
    Are there conflicts that need to be dealt
       with?
    How are we making decisions?

— Friendships

    Do I need to make new friends?
    Do I need to repair or re-establish old
       friendships?

Do I need to maintain close ties with
current friends?
Do I need to share ideas on coping and
options for my future with my friends?
Would it help to draw on others for
support?

— Social groups

Do I want to join new groups?
Church?
Civic?
Neighborhood?
Parents Without Partners?
Self-help?
Can I enhance my own growth by finding
others I can help?

Six months after a wrenching divorce, Clint filled out the Relationships section of his behavioral inventory in the following way:

1. In the space for Spouse/Partner, Clint put a minus. He hated living alone. He felt lonely most of the time and wanted to meet new people.

But at the same time, Clint was afraid of repeating the mistakes he had made with his ex-wife, Kay, in a new relationship. Under Changes Needed, he wrote that he felt he needed to develop better communication skills, specifically that he needed to learn how to allow his marriage partner to participate in decision making — something he had not done in his marriage to Kay.

2. In the area of Family, Clint saw both strengths and weaknesses. The fact that he had three children who loved him as much as he loved them and enjoyed spending time together with him, was a definite plus for him.

On the other hand, taking adequate care of the kids was a

problem. While married, Clint had been pretty much an absentee father — working long hours, traveling frequently, and leaving discipline and nurture to his wife. He had never taken a child to the doctor, for example, and had never been around to mediate in their little disputes. His role was usually that of the heavy-handed authority figure who descended to deal out the rough punishment when things became too much for his wife to handle.

As a result, during the first long weekend that Clint had the kids to himself, they almost drove him up the wall. He decided that Kay had been right — he *had* separated himself too much from the day-to-day parenting responsibilities. He needed to learn effective parenting skills, and so, under Changes Needed he wrote:

> "I need to learn more about disciplining children, and how to care for them better — I don't want to become a 'Hanging Judge' only, nor do I want to become a 'Disneyland Daddy'! I need to find out some fun things we can do together, but also become more involved in meeting their real needs."

3. Because of his work, Clint had not developed an active and involved social life of his own; he had few intimate friends, and those he did have were people he worked with. After the divorce, Clint realized that he had to become more involved socially if he was to meet new people and develop his own social life. He heard about a group called "Parents Without Partners" and wrote under the Changes Needed column:

> "Call the parent group and check into what services they have that I can take advantage of. I need to meet some people who understand the difficulties I'm facing."

He also found it awkward attending the same church his ex-wife attended, so he added:

> "I need to find a new church — maybe one with a good single adults group."

Physical Health

While we discussed this area in detail in Chapter Five, Physical Health is included here so that any decisions you have made can be reinforced and followed up as you integrate them into your new life.

Remember that the components of physical well-being are: exercise, nutrition, rest, and relaxation. Sexual activity can be added to this list as well. Think carefully about each of these as you fill out the following questionnaire, using the " + " and " – " symbols for areas of strength or weakness. Write down the possible changes you might make in any area.

Physical Health

Specific Category	Strengths? or Changes needed?
— Exercise	
Am I exercising regularly?	
Do I need others to exercise with?	
Do I need to make a change in my daily routine because of a new health condition?	
Do I need to learn some exercises I'll enjoy?	
— Nutrition	
Am I eating regular and balanced meals?	
Is my nutrition adequate?	
Do I need to learn how to cook?	
Do I need to learn how to keep good nutrition on a limited budget?	
— Rest/sleep/relaxation	
Do I need to find better ways to relax?	
Am I relying too much on alcohol or other substances to relax?	
Am I having trouble sleeping?	

— Sexuality

　Do I feel comfortable with the sexual
　　aspects of my life right now?
　Do I need to communicate more with my
　　partner about specific needs I have?

— Special considerations

　Do I need to learn new skills?
　　Taking special medications?
　　Giving insulin shots?
　　Adjusting to an artificial limb?
　　Using dialysis?

Todd's crisis began as a result of a sudden collapse at work one day. He was rushed to a hospital, where it was discovered that he suffered from acute hypertension. He allowed that he had not been feeling well for quite some time, but at age thirty-eight did not consider that there could be anything seriously wrong with him. Part of the therapy his doctor recommended was a good, hard look at his lifestyle and counseling to help him lessen the stress that had caused his physical problem.

　The counselor suggested Todd complete a behavioral inventory. Here's the way Todd filled out the Physical Health section of the inventory:

　1. Exercise was an admitted minus for Todd. His basic response to the thought of exercise was to sit quietly in a comfortable chair until the thought went away. He hated the idea of running (said he'd never seen a jogger with a smile on his face!), and he couldn't seem to find time to get involved in activities he might have been more interested in — such as racquetball or tennis. So, in the Changes Neeeded column he wrote:

　　　"Find time to take up a good sport. Maybe an organized class in tennis would help discipline me to stick with it." After a few minutes' thought he added: "Call the

YMCA and see about classes. Also, check into noon workout sessions for executives."

2. In the Nutrition area, Todd found both strengths and weaknesses. Although he knew well which foods were healthful and nutritious for him, and he also enjoyed cooking — both of which were strengths — as part of a two-career family, he nonetheless relied far too much on fast foods and eating out. Since his daily commute to work was long, he most often skipped breakfast and instead had a roll and coffee when he got to the office. Then, lunch at a restaurant near the office, and burgers or fried chicken picked up on the way home from work, or at best, dinner with his wife downtown in the evening. Realizing some changes would be needed, Todd wrote:

> "I know what to do, but I'm just not doing it. I need to help out more with the grocery shopping so that we have good things to cook and eat at home. No more big lunches followed by big dinners. Begin eating lighter meals. No more grease burgers! Bring lunch from home."

3. As Todd had been letting stress build up over the years, his sleep habits had been changing for the worse. His doctor made him realize that he needed good rest, not just more sleep. Alcohol seemed to be the only way he found to unwind, but that in turn wrecked any chance of a good night's sleep. He rated this area a minus and wrote:

> "Cut down on the booze and take a long walk in the evening instead. Find some other, more restful ways to relax."

4. Under the heading of Sexuality, Todd noted a plus. He and his wife enjoyed a close sexual relationship, despite the many handicaps that part of their lives had suffered under of late. He wrote:

> "Let Sue know that she means a lot to me and that I love her very much. Try to add some new sparkle to our lovemaking."

Leisure Activities

During and after a crisis, you may feel that indulging in your regular leisure activities is somehow frivolous or improper. You may feel guilty playing when there is so much serious business to attend to. It is possible to work yourself into such a gloomy mood over your current situation that you cannot even imagine ever having fun again.

Play, however, is one important cornerstone of an active, healthy life, for adults as well as for children. If, because of the crisis event, you have abandoned your normal leisure activities — such as bowling, golf, chess, bridge, tennis, reading, painting, fishing, and so on — you will need to begin finding ways to build play back into your life. If you are one of those people who almost never plays at all, you could begin structuring your new life to include a healthy dose of some leisure activity you find enjoyable.

Read the following questionnaire for the leisure area, thinking about each dimension. Then fill it out as you did the others, using "+" and "−" to rate those areas that are strong and can be left alone and those where work is needed or where definite changes must be made. Then, in the space provided write down any possible changes that come to mind.

Play

	Strengths or
Specific Category	Changes needed?

— Time for play

    Do I take time for play?
    Do I make a point of doing something fun
      regularly each week?

— Playmates

    Do I have others I can enjoy my leisure
      activities with?

Do I have a good time when I am with
them?

— Range of activities

What do I do to play?
Do I need to learn new skills to indulge in
fun activities?
Do I need to develop new interests?

The Play section of the behavioral inventory was the easiest
section for Donald to fill out. He simply had to recall what his
wife and grown children had been telling him for the past
month or so: "Stop mooning around the house and making
yourself depressed. Find something to do with your time.
Now that you're retired, you can do anything you like!"

Although Donald had few activities other than his career as
a school administrator and an occasional game of golf with
a colleague, he had a few ideas. Here's what his inventory
looked like:

1. In the area of Time for Play, Donald marked a big " + "
— he had all the time he wanted, maybe even a little too much.

2. Donald realized he had plenty of potential playmates;
even though he didn't have anyone specific in mind, he knew
that at the club he'd find quite a few people his age to do
things with if he cared to. He rated this area a minus, however,
and wrote under the Changes Needed column:

"Get out and meet some interesting new people. Also,
call up Jack D. and see if he's free in the mornings."

3. Another minus for Donald was in the area of Range of
Activities. After taking a hard look at what he had done over
the past many years in the way of play and leisure activities,
he had to admit that he had never really learned to enjoy his
leisure time. He did enjoy golf, and that was a plus, but he
couldn't see himself becoming a golf nut, playing two rounds
a day for the rest of his life.

His thinking led him back to some of the things he had enjoyed doing a long time ago, to things he had given up in order to concentrate on advancing his career. The wooden playhouse he had built for his preschool children came to mind — also, the fact that he had never done much serious woodworking since then. As he thought about it he realized that he had been collecting tools over the years without really using them, and that maybe his subconscious was trying to tell him something. The more he thought about it, the more excited he became about woodworking. He wrote:

"Check out a few woodworking project books from the library, and take stock of my tools. And ask the kids if they would like me to build a swing set for the grandchildren."

He thought some more and added:

"Go with Marion to her co-ed fitness class. Check out the senior citizens' tennis program she's been talking about. Get involved with her in something."

◆ ◆ ◆

Reading through and filling out the above questionnaires creates a personal inventory that clearly identifies the areas of your life that have been most affected by your crisis, and shows where specific changes can be made. This inventory gives you a picture of what the path ahead can look like.

Now it is time to begin making some of the changes you have considered.

◆ TEN ◆

Making Changes

FOR SOME PEOPLE, simply identifying the areas where change is needed is all they require to get started. These are the same folks who visit a counselor for one session and come away with an idea or two, a new direction, and a spark that unleashes energy for change. This same sort of thing may have happened to you as you went through the last chapter. Simply identifying the fact that you would need to make changes in very specific areas (work, relationships, physical health, play) and looking at the specific headings under each area may have given you ideas about what you should do next. If that's the case with you, great! Go to it!

On the other hand, you might feel swamped as you look over your responses to some of the areas discussed above. You wonder, "How am I ever going to get all of this done?" Just realizing that the crisis affects all of these areas can be overwhelming. But don't give up yet. There are ways to sort through the various adjustments you want to make, and start on a path toward meaningful change. This chapter will detail some tried-and-true principles for behavioral change that grow out of psychotherapy — in particular, behavior therapy. Therapists and counselors use these guidelines all the time in working with their clients. You can apply them to yourself as well.

USE THE INVENTORY TO
CREATE SPECIFIC GOALS

People who have studied the process of behavioral change tell us that you must have some idea of where you are going if you ever hope to get there — a *goal*, in other words. This is what the personal inventory is all about. In filling it out you have been identifying specific changes that need to be made in your life. Now you are one short step away from having goals for your future. For example, if you identified communication with your partner as a possible change, then translate that into a goal: to be able to communicate better with _____ .

Continue right on down the line, translating other problems or weaknesses into goals by using your personal inventory. Try making a list. The main thing is to recognize that over the next many months to several years you have the overall goal of making improvements in the specific areas identified earlier. For example, let's look at how some of the people we discussed earlier translated their Changes Needed into concrete goals.

Todd, the thirty-eight-year-old executive with hypertension, came up with the following goals under the Physical Health section of the inventory:

— develop a regular exercise routine and practice it at least three times a week

— replace heavy business lunches with healthful snacks throughout the day

— learn a good, healthful way to relax

Clint, the recently divorced father of three, wrote down the following goals after examining the Relationships section of his inventory:

— begin dating again in order to meet likely candidates for a long-term relationship

— take a course in marriage and family at the university

— learn better ways to communicate with the opposite sex

— improve my parenting skills

— participate in two or three outside social activities a month

Notice that, in each case, a weakness was translated into a positive goal that when carried out, would help build a new area of strength.

USE YOUR STRENGTHS TO YOUR ADVANTAGE

As we have said earlier, crisis is a time of such upheaval and turmoil that many people forget that they have strengths at all. The executive who is fired from his job doesn't think much about the fact that his body is strong and able — a primary requisite not only for carrying on daily, but for beginning the search for a new position. The woman whose husband recently left her, and whose kids suddenly seem to have become little hellions, dwells so much on this problem that she doesn't remember the fact that she has a good friend who cares about her and a job where she is competent and appreciated.

If you feel out of touch with your strengths, take a little time now to think about them. What do you have going for you? Health? Religious faith? A close friend or two you can call on? A supportive family? A small nest egg?

Identify the strengths in your life right now, and use them to your advantage as you work toward making changes in other areas of your life. If you have friends, ask them to help you — whether it's watching your children while you go for job interviews, or getting the word out that you are looking for work. If you have a small nest egg in the bank that you had been saving for a rainy day, let this be that day; decide now how you might best use it.

The emphasis here is on mobilizing strengths. This is the aftermath of crisis, a time to pull out the stops.

BREAK BIG CHANGES
DOWN INTO SMALL STEPS

This is a basic principle of behavioral change. Few people can make sweeping global changes, but almost anyone can make one small step toward a big change right now. To do this, you have to break the big changes down into smaller, more manageable, units.

Management people in large organizations call this defining objectives. Objectives are those small steps on the way to reaching big goals.

Again, you might even want to make a list of steps that, if taken, would help you reach your goal. If you need a new car, for example, start by writing down the steps or actions that, if taken, bring you closer to your goal of having the car in your driveway. The small steps that lead to accomplishing this big goal include things like:

> — looking through the want ads for cars in your price range
> — visiting two or three dealers to look at their used cars, and exploring the possibility of buying a new one
> — posting a "car wanted" note on the bulletin board in your office
> — telling two or three friends that you are in the market for a car and asking them to keep their eyes and ears open

Notice how each of the foregoing phrases begins: looking, visiting, posting, telling. They are all *action* words.

When you break a big goal into small steps, use action words, since these words prime you to do something about your goals. Even the language you choose to talk about your problems can help or hinder you.

DO A LITTLE BIT EACH DAY, EACH WEEK, EACH MONTH

This follows naturally from the idea of breaking a problem down into small pieces. When you start the day and want to do something to change your life, set your sights on doing one or two of the activities that might help you reach your goal. You may not be able to find a new career in one day, though you might easily do one or more of the following:

— search the want ads in the morning paper
— make two phone calls to personnel offices to ask if they have jobs in your field
— visit one or two companies to complete an application form

Notice how setting your sights on doing something small each day also gives you the experience of success. You are *doing something* about your problems. All the little things that you do can eventually add up to success.

BE SHREWD IN DECIDING WHERE TO START

One of the main things that will be important to you in getting started is keeping your morale up. Granted, for a while you may continue to be depressed, sad, lonely, and all the other negative feelings that go along with a crisis. But when you start trying to make some changes in your life, you want to "play all the angles," so to speak. You want to make it easy not only to succeed, but to keep going. Your best hope is in taking those small, sure steps toward your goal. At the same time you can be shrewd about where and how you start. See if these principles, which counselors use in helping their clients decide how to start on life-change programs, can be helpful to you:

Start on the things that are pinching right now. Ask yourself, "Where does the shoe pinch?" Give that place your earliest attention. Look at all of the changes you identified in your inventory and ask yourself which ones bother you the most right now. It might be that your car is in disrepair, or that your child is having trouble in school, or friends are asking a lot of awkward questions about your spouse who recently moved out. Or it could be that your body feels completely shot, and you are a physical wreck as a result of all the turmoil of the crisis.

Whatever it is, let this pinch be a sign that this area would be a good place for you to start as you think of change in the next many weeks and months.

Start making changes in anything that, if neglected for too long, will reduce your options later. Physical health is an obvious example, since neglect of the body can lead to a breakdown — a cold, flu, or some other illness — that will leave you flat on your back in bed instead of up and around changing your life.

Other examples: A student in crisis who is also facing final exams in two weeks needs to develop a plan for studying (or postponing) exams, since failed courses can ruin grades and wipe out chances for graduate school or prime career placement.

A woman who experiences unbearable anxiety at the thought of leaving the house to go grocery shopping, to interview for a job, or to attend a social function will need to deal with this anxiety before she can move on to other areas of change, since the anxiety prevents her from working on any other goals.

Try killing two birds with one stone. You can keep motivation high by doing any activity that solves two (or more) problems at once. Many times life changes can become bottlenecked around a single major task. When you accomplish that one task, several other smaller activities are suddenly taken care of. It might be that a new job would not only bring in the money you need to take care of monthly expenses (one of your major concerns), but it would also give you social contacts to start meeting new people and thereby improve your social relationships, which is another goal.

GIVE YOUR PEAK HOURS TO YOUR TOP PRIORITIES

Most people have one time during the day when their energy is at a peak. For many people this is in the morning. Others peak in the late afternoon or in the early evening. Therefore, maximize your strengths by tackling the issues you care about most when you are at your best physically and mentally. By working on top priorities in your peak time you increase the chance that you will finish the day having taken successful steps toward your goals.

USE POSITIVE IMAGERY AS A DAILY GUIDE

An essential part of any successful venture — whether starting a large corporation or beginning an exercise program — lies in the ability of the individual to picture success. Presidents of corporations know this, which is why they spend time and money getting their employees to think like winners, to catch the vision of themselves as highly creative, successful people. In fact, the best presidents are those who not only motivate their employees, but also instill in them an image of success.

As noted earlier, it is extremely unlikely that you will succeed if you do not have some kind of positive mental picture or image of what you are trying to achieve. In other words, you can't get someplace if you have no idea where you are going. In the Bible, the Old Testament puts it this way: "Where there is no vision, the people perish" (Proverbs 29:18).

You can apply this concept to your plan for behavioral change. Begin to develop a clear and positive picture of yourself as having worked through the crisis and having emerged at the other end as a happy, satisfied human being who is working, playing, and involved in meaningful relationships.

This is more straightforward than it at first appears; the idea is to conjure up a mental image of yourself as having achieved the goal(s) you are working toward. Picture yourself the way you want to be when you have reached your goal.

One unemployed executive pictured herself as having gone through the process of searching for jobs, interviewing, and landing the job she wanted. She created an image of herself working successfully and happily at that job. A widow whose goal was to return to school to complete her degree in order to get a job as a teacher likewise pictured herself as having completed her education and graduated, and then as working with her students in the classroom. Each person conjured up a vision of what success would be, of themselves as having made it!

Dr. O. Carl Simonton and his colleagues, in their book *Getting Well Again*, suggest the following exercise for creating a positive mental image. You might want to try it.

1. Find a quiet place where you will not be interrupted. Position yourself comfortably on a chair, couch, or bed.

2. Relax your mind and body as much as possible. (Use the relaxation exercises from Chapter Five if that would be helpful.)

3. With your eyes closed, take a deep breath and let it out slowly. Repeat and say the word "relax" to yourself to enhance this state of relaxation.

4. Picture yourself in your current situation, including the events of the day. Notice the problems in your life, and notice any physical reactions you may have as you picture them.

5. Next, review the things in your life that are going well — anything that can be seen as a "plus" — the love of your children, a compliment at work, a good word from a friend, and so on.

6. Now, picture your life after you have made the changes you listed in your personal inventory. Picture yourself as you want to be: employed, or enjoying new friends, or spending meaningful time with your children, or living in a new place. See yourself as going about your daily routine in an easy, comfortable manner, living in your new world. Include as many positive aspects of life as you can think of. Do not try to block out features of your recent crisis. Allow those features to be there, but to remain in the background.

7. Mentally give yourself a "pat on the back" for working toward your goals and for overcoming obstacles.

8. Gradually become aware of your body and its sensations here and now, as you prepare to open your eyes once more. Pay attention to how your body feels.

9. Open your eyes, refreshed, and ready to go about your daily activities.

10. Repeat this exercise periodically — once a day, once every other day, once a week, however often you like. The main thing is to reinforce your positive mental images, to make them a part of your overall program of growth through the crisis.

USE POSITIVE "SELF-TALK" ALONG THE WAY

Along with cultivating a positive mental image, the whole process of establishing yourself in your new world will be greatly enhanced if you develop positive self-talk, too. (You will remember we discussed this in Chapter Eight.) It bears repeating here, for much of your positive motivation can be squelched, and your progress halted, if you allow yourself to entertain hopeless or depressing thoughts.

Repeatedly thinking, for example, "I'm sunk! There's no way out" or "I'm never going to make it" or "It's hopeless. I'll never be able to change" can defeat growth before it has a proper chance to begin. You can replace these negative statements with more balanced, hopeful ones.

Balanced statements take a different perspective and drive it home: "I feel rotten today, but tomorrow could be a whole lot better," or "I didn't find a job today, and I am frustrated as hell. But I did meet some interesting people and maybe I can see them again," or "Changing is the hardest thing I've ever had to do. Still, I don't have to change overnight; I can take it at my own speed."

Notice that these statements do not attempt to deny the negative; instead, they acknowledge it and then move on to include a word of hope for improvement. Clinical experience and research show that this is just the opposite of what most people do when they feel upset. When depressed or upset, people generally concentrate exclusively on the darker side of the situation and block out any awareness of the light. Or they dismiss hopeful possibilities: "The light at the end of the tunnel is probably a train!"

If you do not recognize something good when it is happening to you, you cannot take advantage of it — even though you may want to very badly. The fact is that no one knows exactly what the future will be. It is logically incorrect to assume then that "Things will never get better," or "I'll never get out of this," or "What's the use of trying, it'll never work out."

There is simply no way to know what will work out and what won't. Your best option, therefore, is to remain open to the future, nurturing hope with whatever source is available — whether it is your religious faith, the good example of others, or inspirational literature. Each issue of *Guideposts* magazine and *Reader's Digest* contains many inspirational articles where people just like you have faced and overcome crushing defeats. These people can make good role models, and their insights can speak directly to your situation.

Positive self-talk is actually the foundation of encouragement you build for yourself, and as such it's much more than just looking on the bright side. It is a means of keeping you on track as you learn to make the changes in your behavior and lifestyle necessary to live in your new world. It sets the stage for success.

Such phrases as "I'm just taking things one day at a time," or "I am not there yet, but I have a plan and I know where I'm going," or "Some parts of my life are still pretty bad, but other parts are getting better," or "It is hard, but I am a lot stronger than I thought and I will make it" — these phrases and others like them have all been used by people going through various crises.

You may find a different phrase meaningful. What others find meaningful may strike you as a little trite or clichéd; that's often the case. It doesn't matter; just use whatever words of encouragement speak best to you.

CHART YOUR PROGRESS

As you move through the next weeks and months, learning to live in your new world, it might be helpful to keep track of your progress along the way. This has a double benefit: you can reward yourself for successes and also correct your approach when an activity is not working out as planned — thus keeping you from spinning your wheels and getting frustrated.

Watching yourself move steadily toward your goals will have an edifying effect all its own. As you see yourself adjusting, adapting, and growing, you will become even more encouraged and confident.

You might want to keep a notebook or journal to record your progress. Your first entry could be a photocopy of the behavioral inventory from Chapter Nine. A good appointment book — one with enough space to write in not only daily and weekly plans, but also monthly objectives and longer term goals — can be very helpful.

Two other suggestions will help you keep track of your continued growth and improvement:

• At least once a month, take a look at your personal inventory and note the progress that is being made. Put a check mark by an item once you have done something to work on it. Later you can put a line through it, or a star on it, to show that you have accomplished it.

During these monthly review sessions you can also add to the inventory any items you may have remembered or discovered in the previous month. Write this new item in a different colored ink, or put a date by it to show it was added later.

• Invite a friend to work with you. A friend who knows you well can serve as a sort of reality check and also give moral support as you make the changes necessary for living in a world changed by crisis. It might be especially helpful to set up a "contract," for example, to meet "every Wednesday at 4:00 at Louie's Coffee Shop" to talk over how you're doing and how to use the ideas from this chapter.

• Take credit for your successes. Remember to reward yourself whenever you accomplish one of your goals. Recognize when you have made a significant move toward your objectives, and celebrate that fact in some way.

OVERCOMING OBSTACLES

As with any new endeavor, there will be times when things don't work out, when you don't reach your objectives, when you don't feel motivated, when the pace slows or comes to a halt. It happens. When it does, it seems like all the hard work you have done has been wasted effort. You realize you need to get back on track, but how?

There are three questions you can ask yourself when obstacles arise in your path:

1. *"Have I missed something?"* Maybe it is information you lack, a new skill you need to develop, or a risk you need to take in order to proceed. In other words, some additional input is required to get things moving again. It may be that you have misjudged the nature of the change you are making or have missed some important aspect of your situation that is making it difficult for you to proceed.

Suzanne, for example, in trying to manage two small children and hold down a full-time job as a single parent, seemed to get more and more overwhelmed by the chaos that daily life had become. She assumed that she ought to be able to handle dealing with her children easily, but every little problem turned into a test of her self-sufficiency. Her assumptions about child-rearing, she soon discovered, had serious flaws. Something more was needed.

Finally, after one nasty episode with the children, she came away admitting that she couldn't do it alone, that there was no one she had to prove herself to as a mother, and that it would not be a weakness for her to admit that she needed help in handling her two active youngsters. Swallowing her pride, she called a local child-guidance center and asked for help.

After enrolling in a program for single parents, Suzanne learned that she was no different than many other single mothers who also worked, and more important, that there were certain skills she could learn that would make her task as a mother much more satisfying and gratifying. Setting out to acquire those new skills became the turning point for her.

2. *"Do I really want to change?"* It may be that for all your outward determination and willingness to adapt to your new world, inwardly you are very comfortable living just as you are. There may be certain benefits to your present situation that you have not acknowledged to yourself. If you appear helpless or ill, you get more attention from people, and you have an excuse for not confronting your responsibilities.

It may be, too, that you have undertaken a change (or adopted a goal) for the wrong reason; your inner self is telling you that you do not really want to change. Like many others, you may have approached a change as "something I should do" for the family or because it is expected. You feel you *should* begin looking for a different job, or you *should* be exercising and eating better.

The problem with doing things because you *should* do them is that it hardly ever works. Every time you tell yourself "I should," an inner voice responds with "I will not." When this happens, an inner battle is set up that never can be won. You may go through the motions, but real accomplishment never gets any nearer.

This is exactly what happened to Paula when she found herself floundering in her attempts to develop a life of her own after moving to a new city. She had moved to a large southwestern metropolitan area directly after she left college. A large part of her reason for moving was to get away from her mother, with whom she had had bitter battles all through college. Paula wanted nothing more than to make it on her own; however, nothing she did went according to plan.

Try as she might she could not seem to meet any new friends, and the people she did meet she didn't feel comfortable with. She wasn't happy in her apartment — a single-bedroom unit in an impersonal high-rise building. She found herself picking fights with her brother and his wife, who also lived in the city and were Paula's chief social contact. In short, the energy and excitement she had experienced in high school and college dissipated, and she found herself retreating each evening to her apartment with a bottle of wine.

As a last resort, her brother recommended a counselor and made an appointment for her. She went, and then continued with sessions on her own. During one of the sessions, Paula spoke drearily of all the things she knew she should do; she should get her apartment fixed up a little; she should get out and meet some new people; she should start exercising; she should start dieting and lose some weight; she should work at being happier at her job . . .

The counselor allowed her to talk about these things for a while and then asked Paula whose voice she heard behind all these "shoulds." Paula paused only a moment and then declared, "My mother's!"

Although Paula wanted many of the things on her "should" list, she had never given herself a chance to make them her own. As soon as the *should* thought occurred, it triggered in Paula the idea that it was something her mother wanted, and psychologically she rebelled against it. In refusing to give in to her "inner mother," however, she was wrecking her own life.

The breakthrough came when Paula recognized that she was far better off working with her own desires, instead of getting into an inner conflict with her mother. She took a new approach and found that it worked well for her. Every time she caught herself saying, "I should," she simply backtracked and asked herself, "What would *I like* to do, regardless of what anybody says I *should* do?" She began taking control of her own life.

If you find yourself in a similar situation, stuck with an inner voice telling you what you "should" be doing, start asking yourself seriously, "What do I really *want* to do? What are the benefits of my situation now? What will the benefits be if I change?" Allow yourself to be realistic about the gains and losses in moving out of your present situation. Question your own motives until you can come up with good, solid reasons for changing — reasons that make sense to you, that represent some real gain for you.

3. *"Are my goals unreasonable?"* If you find yourself continually falling short in your efforts to reach a goal, it may be that your goal is too high or, paradoxically, not high enough. Set a goal too high and it will be difficult to keep yourself motivated to reach it, because deep inside you know that you'll never get there; too low and you know that, once it is achieved, it won't make any real difference in your life.

Deciding whether goals are reasonable is not difficult, but it requires a certain objectivity. It may be that a close friend, your minister, or a counselor can supply the needed objectivity if you are having trouble finding it yourself.

Of course, it need not be that the goal is unreasonable at all. You may simply be trying too hard to reach it, or trying to reach it too quickly. Or, again, not trying hard enough. In any case, the result is the same: progress is thwarted.

If, in looking at your daily schedule, you see that you are trying to do too much, back off a bit; take it slower. If you are not attempting enough to keep life interesting, add another item or two to your list, make a small challenge for yourself daily that can spur you on. In other words, mix it up a bit. Try something new.

PUTTING CHANGE IN PERSPECTIVE

Throughout this chapter we have examined various approaches and methods of adapting to and adjusting to a new life in a new world — your world after the crisis. No matter how you say it, adapting and adjusting mean change, and change is never easy. Any crisis demands changes of one kind or another. The question is, however, will the changes be toward growth or toward debilitation?

We have discussed at length the idea that in order for growth to occur you need to "do something about it!" This can mean taking the initiative, looking ahead, setting up challenges, motivating yourself, identifying goals, setting objectives, making plans, and charting progress.

All of this is heavily weighted toward the "how-to" aspect of growth. And it is valid.

There is, however, another equally valid idea about growth and change that we would like to mention as a way of wrapping up this section of the book — the idea that growth happens in its own good time.

This idea might seem contradictory in light of all we have said thus far, but not really — not if we let it lend perspective to all the various methods and approaches we have touched on. Recognizing that we cannot force growth to take place, that wounds take their own time to heal, that life has a rhythm of its own — and, at the same time, that in order to grow we need to provide the right conditions for it to happen, that wounds can be bound up so that they heal more quickly, that the rhythm of life can be enhanced — recognizing all this can allow us to approach the matter of growth and change in a more mature and balanced way.

Balance is what we're after: not waiting too long for growth to take place, nor trying to hurry it too fast.

Growth following crisis can show itself in the learning of new skills, in the adjustments you make to your new life, in new activities, in new relationships, in new and better ways to take care of your body, in more exciting ways to use your leisure time, in more satisfying ways to work. This is the phoenix factor: new life can rise from the ashes of the old.

· ELEVEN ·

A Child in Crisis:
How Adults Can Help

MANY ADULTS who are working through a crisis are often far more worried about how their children are weathering the storm than they are about themselves. They say things like: "I'll make it, but what about my five-year-old?" Or "I don't want Johnny to be scarred for life."

Children experience crisis in much the same way as adults — they see their lives turned upside-down, have powerful and painful emotions, and experience overwhelming turmoil and confusion when their world collapses. Children need the help of a parent or other adult to understand the meaning of events, to work through thoughts and feelings, and to take the behavioral steps that move them along the path toward growth. As a matter of fact, children watch adults during a time of crisis to find out how to act, think, and feel.

The message of this chapter is a hopeful one: you can help your own children during intense crisis by guiding them through their own version of the crisis-resolution principles we have described. And though the danger for children in a crisis is that they may get lost on a developmental detour, the opportunity is that they may just as easily experience developmental leaps, growing in maturity and in understanding themselves and the world around them.

RESOLVING CHILDREN'S CRISES

You may want to have a look at the charts for developmental and situational crises (found in Appendixes A and B). Notice the range of crises that can occur during childhood — they include everything from illness and injury to the risks children undertake when testing limits in the world around them. Many times situational crises such as migration, conflicts with parents and teachers, changes in schools, and so on are outward manifestations of children's trying to work through normal developmental issues (listed in the third column of the developmental chart of Appendix A as tasks or preoccupations).

The main concern for adults in helping children in crisis lies in the cognitive dimension, or what the child is *learning* during the crisis. With every major crisis that occurs during the life of a child, parents and caregivers can open the door to growth by looking closely at what the child is learning from the experience, and then by taking steps to influence what is learned.

The fact is, whether we make any special intervention or not, children *will* learn important lessons about life through every childhood crisis they experience. Our questions need to be: What are they learning? How are they interpreting events, including their own frustration and emotional pain? Are the conclusions they draw the ones that will move them on a path toward strength and health as adults, or toward withdrawal from life?

Building on the learning theme, let's look at how to help a child touch each of the four bases described in Chapter Four in resolving a crisis.

First Base: Physical Survival and Well-Being
A child faces essentially the same threats to life and limb that an adult does during a crisis. Anxiety and worry about

whether Mommy or Daddy will get back together, for example, can show themselves in stomachaches, headaches, sleeplessness, and a variety of other physical symptoms. And, just like adults, children are susceptible to life-threatening behavior: Until recently, many thought that suicide was only a remote possibility for children under ten, though we now know that this is not the case at all. Troubled youngsters can view death as a solution to seemingly insurmountable problems and are capable of carrying out death wishes.

The best protection for the life of a child going through a crisis is to listen for indications that the child has any thoughts about the circumstances' being so hopeless that ending life might be a solution, and then follow the principles outlined in "Protecting Against Fatal Moves" in Chapter Three. Verbal and nonverbal clues should be followed by direct inquiry from a parent or guardian, teacher, or any other adult in a position to help.

For example, you might say: "You said that sometimes you felt like you wanted to die. What do you mean by that?" If an intention or thought about hurting oneself is combined with any sort of plan and a means to carry it out, then the situation should be brought to the attention of a professional helper, such as a physician, counselor, or therapist. (See Appendix C, "Getting Outside Help.")

In most cases, however, the main efforts of crisis resolution will not be in the prevention of suicide, but in helping the child cope with the physical distress of a crisis. Again, the guidelines for adults (Chapter Five, "Taking Care of Your Body") apply directly to children as well.

Since most children are unable to take complete responsibility for their own physical health, it is up to adults to provide guidance. Remember, your child needs the same balance in life that you do: exercise, rest, and nutrition.

Many children's games, in addition to providing a direct opportunity for exercise and relaxation, can also give adults a chance to make good contact with a child during times of extreme stress. Playing catch, riding bicycles, taking a walk, flying a kite — all can become mini-vacations from immediate pressures, and also provide much needed exercise.

Helping children follow good nutritional patterns during a crisis might be the toughest job a parent faces, and expectations should be set at a realistic level. In many cases you should expect some tradeoffs. For example, it could be that your child's favorite junk-food cereal will provide a special comfort during a time of intense turmoil; even though the nutritional value of the cereal is not high, its "comfort quotient" makes it an acceptable temporary substitute.

The main areas to watch nutritionally are sugar, caffeine, and nonnutritive additives present in many processed foods that appeal to children. All can increase the stress and tension that children feel during a crisis. You will have to use your own creativity to lend a balance between foods that appeal to your child and those that provide healthful nutrition.

Clinical experience with children has demonstrated that they can easily be taught the relaxation techniques in Chapter Five. For many children the deep-muscle relaxation steps can be integrated into a bedtime routine — combined with a soothing story or bedtime prayers. Be careful not to set your expectations too high on a child's mastering relaxation skills immediately, but look for ways to facilitate relaxation in the weeks and months following a crisis event.

In the aftermath of any crisis, the focus of learning for children should be on the effects of the crisis on their bodies. They should be told that the unusual events they are experiencing have an effect on how they feel, and that special steps need to be taken to insure continued good health. Your own reassuring words can help a child understand that he is not abnormal for having a stomachache, or for not being able to sleep because he is thinking about Daddy who is ill, or a friend who moved away, or Grandma who died, and so on. Your message should be: "Yes, it's normal. Our bodies react to things that happen around us. Let's do what we can to take care of ourselves right now and in the weeks ahead."

All in all, follow the very same guidelines for children that are described for adults in Chapter Five, though look for special ways to create a child's version that works for a younger person.

Second Base: Managing Painful Feelings

During a crisis, emotions run high, adding to the overall confusion of the experience. If this is true for adults who have had long practice in dealing with their feelings, it is doubly true for children, who are apt to experience emotions they have never felt before: grief, extreme anxiety, intense frustration, fear.

A child of seven who moves from a home in South Dakota to another in Kansas may experience overwhelming feelings of anxiety as he enrolls in a new school in a completely different social and physical environment. The teachers and students are different, the climate is different — even the books are different! This can produce a crisis for the youngster as potent as any migration crisis an adult can experience.

Helping a child manage painful feelings during a crisis presents a special opportunity for parents and other adult caregivers to open the door for positive contact and growth. A child can be helped to express his or her feelings and to deal with them appropriately.

Begin by reminding yourself that children have feelings too! Often, in the midst of a crisis affecting the whole family — unemployment of the breadwinner, death of a loved one, a severe accident, divorce — adults tend to forget that children experience intense feelings similar to their own. In fact, during a crisis children look to the adults around them for guidance to see what to do with these feelings. If, for instance, Mom and Dad tuck away angry feelings during a divorce, pretending that nothing is happening, a child is left with the conclusion that she is abnormal if she feels angry.

What goes on in a little one's mind is something like this: "Something must be wrong with me. Here I feel scared and angry and all mixed up, and no one else is upset at all. It must be my fault."

There is no single best way to help children manage painful emotions; each child expresses emotions differently, and parents need to be sensitive to the way their child chooses. Some children will be more private with their feelings, expressing them symbolically. Others can be encouraged to talk about what they are feeling and will open up easily.

The point is not so much *how* children express their feelings, or when they express them, or to whom, but that they do find some way to give expression to what is going on inside them.

The best approach for helping a child deal with painful feelings is for the adults closest to him to own up to their own painful emotions during the crisis (or to identify how they have felt in similar situations), and to put their feelings into words that the child can understand.

Following the death of a loved one, for example, a parent might say, "I am so sad that Grandma died. I sure do miss her already." Simple yet sensitive statements like this show how the adult is feeling, and leave room for a child to start putting his or her feelings into words — like, "I miss Grandma, too, and that makes me real sad."

On other occasions it will be necessary to observe how the child is talking, how he is behaving in order to discover what he is feeling. A child who hurls a book down violently, or unexpectedly throws a tantrum over a favorite toy, may well be upset about more than the surface event. Similarly, a child who has no energy to do anything, or refuses to participate in favorite play activity, may be stuck on troublesome or depressing thoughts.

In cases like these it is often helpful to prime the pump, so to speak, by gently commenting on what is happening, using reflective, nondirective statements like: "It seems like you're upset today." Or "I can imagine how angry you must feel."

Anything the parent can do to give a child accurate words to describe a feeling will be helpful. It gives a verbal handle — angry, sad, depressed, lonely — to an upsetting state of affairs, and it suggests to a child that emotions are acceptable. The aim is to induce some form of expression for these feelings and to bring understanding. Just as with adults, children need to vent anger and frustration in acceptable ways: to kick a ball, to hit a pillow, to cry and let the tears flow so that reassurance can follow.

Reassurance is important to children; they need to feel that though this one area of life is rocky at present, other areas are stable. This gives parents and other caring adults a twofold objective in helping a child manage painful feelings: (1) to enable expression of negative feelings and (2) to offer reassurance and comfort.

If either aspect is ignored, a child can feel insecure and fearful of the future. In other words, if feelings are not expressed, they may interfere with other areas of life — in relationships with friends, in the ability to concentrate in school or to sleep. Similarly, if a child expresses painful feelings, but no reassurance is forthcoming, then the feelings take over a much larger portion of the child's energy than they should and affect other areas of life.

Once again, our watchword for children is *learning*. The guidance we offer to help children learn to identify and express the feelings that seem strange, new, and frightening will eventually help them deal with similar situations on their own in later life.

Third Base: Changing the Mind
Children begin very early in life to form mental pictures, develop beliefs, and make statements about the world. Even

though young children do not yet possess the accumulated factual knowledge or reasoning abilities of a full-grown adult, the actual process of interpreting events in the world around them and then feeling and acting accordingly is exactly the same as for an adult.

When a child experiences a crisis, either directly or indirectly as a member of a family that is undergoing a crisis, it is up to the parent or adult caregiver to (1) find out what the child believes about what happened, and if necessary (2), provide additional information or alternative interpretations about what happened.

A child involved in divorce, for example, often believes that her parents' separation is her fault, that if she had not been naughty Mommy and Daddy would have stayed together and everything would be fine. These beliefs, though erroneous, are logical from the child's point of view. It is up to the parent to set the record straight and to help the child form a more accurate picture of how the divorce came about and how to interpret it.

One of the best ways to accomplish this is to listen to what children say when they talk about crisis-related matters, paying particular attention to the *meaning* they give to events. You can also look for an opportunity to ask a few nonthreatening, open-ended questions, listening carefully to the answers. When a clear picture of what the child believes about what happened emerges, the adult can assess whether the child's beliefs are accurate or inaccurate and then offer new information or an alternative interpretation of an unsettling event.

This could mean literally supplying sentences, phrases, concepts, pictures, and explanations that are both true to what happened and that allow the child to face the future constructively. (Note, this principle, explained in Chapter Seven, is exactly the same for the child as for the adult in this respect.)

Using the divorce example once again, it might go something like this: "No, Heather, it isn't your fault that Mommy and Daddy aren't living together anymore. We are going to be living apart from now on. It's because we have been fighting and arguing so much that we think this is better. Both of us still love you very much, and no matter what happens nothing will change that."

Most situational crises — unemployment of a parent, death of a loved one or friend — will touch off a whole host of questions from children. In a situation where a close relative or friend dies, either after a long illness or as a result of a tragic accident, your own eight-year-old daughter might, at some time or another, ask herself questions like the following:
"What is it like to die?"
"What does it feel like to be dead?"
"What happens at the funeral home?"
"What does a dead person look like?"
"What will happen when I die?"
"Is there really a heaven?"
"If I get sick, will I die too?"
"Whose fault is it?"
"Why are some people crying, and others not crying?"
Children ask themselves these questions in their own minds regardless of whether we participate in this process. And they draw conclusions, sometimes based on false information. If misperceptions are not corrected, children will move through and past a crisis and on into adulthood acting on erroneous information.

As you supply children with information during times of crisis, let the following guide you:

Be sure to answer their questions, not yours. In other words, provide information sufficient for the child's question at that time, not more than he or she needs to hear. A four-year-old might ask: "What happens when a person dies?" Further inquiry might indicate that the child is concerned primarily about what happens to the physical body — leading you to provide brief information about the body being put in the casket and then in the ground — instead of a long, abstract philosophical treatise on whether or not there is life after death. If you are in doubt, ask the child a few questions yourself to see exactly what he or she wants to know at the time.

Tell the truth. Few children emerge from crisis situations better off for being told untruths. Remember that for children, as for adults, something in their world has been shattered by the crisis. Their way of looking at that world has broken down. They need to reconstruct the world, and in some cases add awarenesses or thoughts or constructs to an area of life that they simply hadn't thought about before. Our task is to equip them with ideas and concepts. It is better to tell a young child that Grandpa, whom the child sees in the casket, is dead, and that the body is no longer working, than to euphemistically reply, "Grandpa is sleeping." Sleeping is both untrue and confusing to a little boy who goes to sleep every night himself.

This tell-the-truth principle applies to our choice of words as well. Just as in sex education it is better to teach children the proper anatomical words for the different parts of their bodies, it is better in dealing with a crisis to use words that are understandable and accurate.

If you choose to tell a child that someone has "passed on" instead of "died," prepare yourself to define further (if the child asks) what "passing on" means. You may use both. Depending upon your theology, the body may be dead, though a person's soul or spirit may pass on to another life. Notice that whatever you say will be an individual decision, based on your own view of the world. This is your opportunity to teach your own child what you believe to be true and to prepare your child to go on living in light of that truth.

Balance harsh reality with hope. Children can be devastated or overwhelmed by some harsh truths during times of crisis. For instance, Mommy and Daddy will no longer live together; Aunt Sue is dead; Tommy moved away to California and is not coming back; Daddy had a terrible accident at work and doesn't have an arm anymore . . . and so on.

A child needs to hear concepts that both explain the negative fact that he has just been exposed to, but that also put that negative fact in the context of a hopeful future.

This is not the same as looking at the future through rose-colored glasses; rather it is broadening the perspective to include other, more hopeful, realities for a child, along with the negative realities.

For example, "Mommy and Daddy will not be living together anymore, but we love you very much, and we will each spend a lot of time with you." In such a statement you are adding another reality, a hopeful reality, to the negative reality of divorce.

It's important to remember that every loss for a child should be balanced with some hopeful idea that life will go on in the future.

If a dear friend moves away, we want the child to understand both that yes, the friend is moving away, *but* that you will also be able to write to him, and maybe have him come to visit you sometime next year. From a cognitive point of view you want the child to understand that both things are true: Johnny moved, *and* he is still your friend, and you can maintain contact with him.

The same principle of balancing the negative reality with the hopeful future can be applied to all crises that children face. Even in the most devastating circumstances — as when a sibling or a parent dies — the harsh reality can be balanced with the loving support that a friend or relative can provide.

Home Plate: Adjusting Behavior

The task of adjusting behavior in children is quite similar to the previous task of changing the mind, only here, instead of working with ideas and concepts, we are working with concrete behaviors. The adult role is much the same: identify what behaviors or skills a child needs to accomplish the developmental transition or crisis, and then teach these behaviors or skills.

This teaching can take the form of modeled behavior — in which you or someone else *shows* what to do or how to act.

Actually, children are learning all the time from adults around them; they imitate parents and others naturally. For better or worse, they learn by the example we set. This holds true for the biggest area of behavioral adjustment for children: learning to relate to peers, particularly how to resolve conflict.

Children see how adults act toward one another in conflict situations, and they turn around and imitate this behavior when they find themselves in similar situations. Thus, if we want children to learn how to share, or take turns, we must be very deliberate in our own behavior. We must demonstrate how a person who shares his things behaves in real-life situations.

Beyond this, parents can help initiate actions that help children adjust. A good example might be when the family moves and a child loses a close friend. In this situation a child needs to learn how to say goodbye, to express feelings of sadness, and to engage in behaviors that allow the child to maintain contact through phone calls, visits, or letters — these are simple behavioral steps a child can take to make the transition of losing a friend more bearable, and learn something in the process: how to say goodbye and maintain a friendship, and more important, how to go on living in a new world. This is, after all, the heart of the resolution process.

Think back to the behavioral checklist for adults in Chapter Nine, "Adjusting Your Behavior." Picture your child in the new world she finds herself in after a crisis, and in particular, ask yourself what new behaviors your child will need in terms of work (school), play, relationships with other people, and health. Identify the behaviors needed to live in this new world, and then set about to teach your child the new behaviors.

For example, a boy who moves across the country in the middle of a school year, let's say the third grade, comes into a brand-new school in the middle of the fall term. He suddenly finds that everybody else is way ahead of him in math, and that the favorite sport here is soccer, not football. It would make a lot of sense for his parents to find some way to get special tutoring in math (or do it themselves) and to help the youngster learn something about soccer. The behavior of performing math at a particular level and fitting in with others in terms of sports could be critical in the child's adjustment to this new world.

Similarly, a child may need to learn to give himself insulin shots, or to manage an artificial limb, as a part of the resolution process for a crisis related to illness or injury.

For instance, Suzie, a little girl who lost an eye to cancer during her first year, had to adjust to her new plastic eye. To her parents' dismay (at the time, though later remembered with laughter), the twenty-month-old began taking her artificial eye out at odd times: while sitting in the cart at the grocery store, or while watching TV with her friends. Suzie's parents soon realized that they needed to teach her appropriate behavior — that the eye was only to be taken out "at home, when we clean it, upstairs in the bathroom before bedtime." Later on, she learned to take care of her own plastic eye, and how to protect her one good eye.

WEAR A CHILD'S SHOES

The four principles of crisis resolution are essentially the same for children as for adults — we simply have to consider a child's version of each. Put yourself in your child's shoes. Look *up* at the world (you're shorter now if you are in her shoes), and see how you feel, how you interpret the world, and in particular, what new skills you will need to make it in this new world, whether a world changed by divorce, unemployment of a father, injury, migration, or whatever.

Once you understand the situation from a child's point of view, use your immense influence as a parent — or teacher, childcare worker, babysitter. Remember, you're a chief model, a resource of ideas, and a coach for behavior. You can help a child take care of his or her body, identify and express feelings, develop true and hopeful understandings of the situation and the future, and make the concrete changes in behavior necessary for growth.

· TWELVE ·

Putting It All Together

ALL OF OUR DISCUSSION of surviving and growing through a crisis is based on two main principles: (1) there are four bases to touch in growing through a crisis and (2) there is a way to measure whether or not you have touched them.

In other words, by covering the four life areas outlined in this book you can grow through a crisis; this growth is a direct function of how you take care of your body, manage painful feelings, change your thoughts and attitudes, and adjust your behavior. What is more, growth can be measured — you can tell if you're progressing toward a new life.

This second point — measuring your progress or knowing whether you're growing in all four areas — is something many people have questions about at this stage. This chapter will answer these questions, as well as a few others people generally ask about crisis resolution.

HOW CAN I TELL IF I AM PROGRESSING?

Look for improvement in each of the four areas: taking care of your body, managing feelings, changing your attitudes to face the future, and making behavioral adjustments to live in a new environment. Monitor your *activity* to see that you are doing something good for yourself in each area.

You know you are working through the crisis in a growing, healthful way if you find that you are practicing better health habits on a daily basis; if you have identified your feelings and found appropriate ways to express them, and notice that they have less of a hold over you, that you understand them better; if you are finding answers to your questions about the crisis, its impact on you and your future, and you begin to understand *why* the event was so upsetting to you; if you are developing an image of yourself as living in the future in a positive and productive way, a view that recognizes what happened and at the same time looks forward with hope; if you can point to concrete steps you have taken to keep yourself working, to improve your relationships with others around you, and to make your leisure time meaningful and relaxing.

HOW CAN I TELL IF I HAVE COMPLETED THE PROCESS?

You know you have successfully resolved the crisis when the crisis event has been woven into the fabric of your life in such a way that you are ready to face the future and get on with the business of living.

By the same token, you know that you are *not* yet finished if you are blocking the crisis event and its aftermath out of your awareness, pretending that it did not happen, or somehow denying its existence. While blocking it out, or denying it, is often part of the *early* reaction to a crisis event, for growth to occur you must move beyond this reaction to recognize what happened and what it means to you.

You also know that the resolution process is unfinished if you have closed down one or more areas of your life because of the crisis: if you have withdrawn from close relationships, find yourself unable to work, have difficulty in finding any enjoyment in life, experience severe behavioral symptoms (being unable to leave the house for fear that something bad might happen, for instance), or continue to have physical complaints related to the onset of the crisis (disruptions in sleep, sexual difficulties, headaches, or ulcers).

Growth can occur when the crisis event can take its place right alongside other events in your life — this is what it means for the crisis to be woven into the fabric of life.

Earlier, we suggested thinking of life as a huge quilt or tapestry with various designs representing your life experiences — good as well as bad. While a bad experience may color your whole perception of the tapestry, once you get beyond it you can see that the bad experience has become a part of the overall design. It is not so persistent in your mind, not so "ever present." It may even look very small. You can point to it and remember it, but its presence does not ruin the tapestry; rather, it adds to the overall design.

There is a big difference in people who have integrated the crisis event into their lives and those who have not. Those who have are looking ahead; those who have not are directing their main energies backward toward the past.

In order to answer the question "How do I know when I have completed the process?" ask yourself these other questions: Am I ready to face the future? Can I work, play, engage in loving and rewarding relationships, and take care of myself physically?

A "yes" answer to these questions is a sign of healthy resolution of a crisis. You have made progress. What is more, you have likely grown in the process.

WHAT IF I CANNOT FACE THE FUTURE?

If, after many months, you find yourself closed to the future, dreading each new day and unable to function normally at work, at play, or in your personal relationships, or to take care of yourself adequately, then you need to reassess the situation. Simply put, if you are not yet where you should be, then you need to check to see if you have touched all the bases in working through the crisis.

You might begin by asking yourself a few questions:

• Have I done all I can to take care of my body? Am I exercising, finding ways to relax, eating properly? (First base — review Chapter Five.)

• Are there feelings I have not expressed that might be standing in the way of my moving into the future? Am I holding on to anger, bitterness, resentment, guilt, or some other negative emotion? Do I have unexpressed fears about my future? (Second base — review Chapter Six.)

• Do I know what the crisis means to me? Is a lack of insight or information standing in my way? Do I have all the facts? Do I still have unanswered questions? Do I understand what the crisis did to my big beliefs? Am I equipped mentally to face the future? Can I even imagine a satisfying life for myself in the future? (Third base — review Chapters Seven and Eight.)

• Have I made concrete changes in my behavior that allow me to live in my new world? Have I adjusted to new ways of working, spending leisure time, developing loving relationships, and taking care of my body? Am I creating a new and satisfying lifestyle for myself? (Home plate — review Chapters Nine and Ten.)

If, in reviewing these questions, you find one or more areas where you need to do some more work, double-check each of the tasks and see what needs to be done. Then, make a special effort to follow through, or find someone to help you work through the remaining tasks. (See Appendix C, "Getting Outside Help.")

HOW LONG SHOULD IT TAKE
TO WORK THROUGH A CRISIS?

Those who have studied crises say that the initial pain, confusion, and disorganization are frequently over in a matter of weeks (usually six or so). After this phase passes, you will begin to put yourself back together one way or another, to develop a new stability. You will find some way to start sleeping again, perhaps, or begin eating regularly once more, or some way to keep emotions like grief or anger under control.

We human beings are complex organisms that require a more or less steady state to function properly. After a traumatic blow, our systems demand that we get back to a steady state relatively soon. This steady state, however, may not be one that is good for us, and in fact it may be downright harmful over time.

The point is that even though the outward symptoms have gone away — the tears or bouts of rage have stopped, or sleep is no longer frequently interrupted, or you are eating regularly once more — it does not mean the crisis has been resolved. Usually, it takes anywhere from several months to several years to work through a crisis properly. (We say months to years because people differ so widely that we really cannot be any more precise than this.)

For some people, a matter of months will be all it takes to recover. For others, the process of recovering emotionally, thinking things through, and making behavioral changes that show payoff will be much slower. There is basically no "normal" time frame for working through a crisis — it all depends on the person involved and the nature of the crisis.

CAN I TELL WHAT STAGE
OF THE CRISIS I AM IN?

Because the research on crisis stages is very confusing, we have talked very little about stages or phases of crisis in this book.

The consistency of thought needed to make definite statements about crisis stages is simply not available. Still, it has been noted that people do move through various phases during a crisis, at least four of which we can identify. A person's initial reaction to a crisis event can be one of two types: *outcry* or *denial*. Some people react with an almost reflexive emotional outpouring that can include weeping, panic, screaming, confusion. Others do not react at all; they may even act as if nothing happened. For the moment, they somehow deny the reality of what has just happened. It may be that they need to put aside their reactions in order to help others in distress — as in a natural disaster or emergency. Denial serves to block out the pain and panic in order to deal with more immediate issues, such as saving oneself or saving others.

In the next phase of crisis most people alternate back and forth between denial and *intrusiveness* — sometimes blocking the event out of awareness, and other times being inundated with thoughts and images and fears about what has happened. The intrusiveness stage is one that is characterized by a great deal of disorganization — inability to sleep, to concentrate, and to eat, frictions with friends and family members, and so on.

The next phase — *working through* the crisis — involves dealing with the thoughts, feelings, and behavioral adjustments associated with getting through the crisis, moving past it and into the future.

The last phase, *completion,* refers to the time when the crisis event becomes woven into the fabric of life, and the crisis experience is left behind.

Perhaps the most useful way to consider the stages is to remind yourself that in the early phases (outcry, denial, intrusiveness), your primary concern will be physical survival (First base, in other words) and dealing with disruptive emotions. Consider progress in the other two areas (changing attitudes

The Stages of Crisis

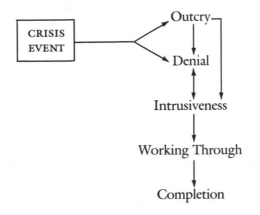

(Source: "Diagnosis and Treatment of Stress Response Syndromes: General Principles" by M. J. Horowitz, in *Emergency and Disaster Management*, edited by H. J. Parad, H. L. P. Resnik, and L. G. Parad [Bowie, Maryland: The Charles Press Publishers, Inc., 1976]. Reprinted by permission.)

and adjusting behavior) as optional or extra. Your primary concern initially is simply to survive the experience. As these early weeks pass, however, you will begin giving more attention to the other three areas as well.

Our advice is to think more about touching the four bases than about the stage you may be in at any given time. In the weeks and months following the event that has thrown you into crisis, let your concern be to begin working in some way, at your own pace, on the four areas we've described.

Remember that, under our rules, crisis resolution differs from the game of baseball, where you hit the ball and then have to run the bases in the correct order and reach home plate to make a score. In our game, you can run from one base to another and back again, touching any base you can in any order you desire: you can go from home to second, then to third, across to first and back to second. Or you can sit out in the dugout for a while, pitch if you want to, or take a turn at bat. No umpire will call you out, no coach will tell you how to run the bases. The only rule is that you must touch all the bases sometime during the game.

WILL I HAVE RELAPSES?

Most crises bring with them a number of marker events — special dates, memories, anything that reminds you of the trauma you've suffered. These marker events have the potential for producing deep depression, almost like a mini-crisis. Some people, for instance, report feeling depressed at the one-year anniversary of a divorce, a time of vulnerability when they feel a special press to remarry.

In the first twelve months following any crisis event, every single thing you do will be for the "first time" — the first time you have done it in your new post-crisis world. For example, it will be the first time you have Christmas without your loved one, the first time you give your child a birthday party without Daddy's being there, the first time you go out on a date as a divorced adult.

Each of these "firsts" can be expected to remind you of the crisis you have experienced. Perhaps more than remind you — the whole thing can get revved up again in your mind and heart to where you feel the terrible pain all over again. This can happen for years afterward, too, depending upon the intensity of the original crisis and what it meant to you.

As time passes, however, the intensity will fade, and feelings will eventually mellow — especially as you make progress in the four areas we've been talking about. During the first twelve months or so, you can expect many times when things fall apart, when it doesn't seem as if you've made any progress at all. There will be times when you start crying all over again, or get boiling mad, or nervous, or fearful. If you happen to be the sort of person who has very high expectations, you may be overly critical of yourself, wondering whether you have made any progress at all. But be gentle with yourself, save your self-criticism, and concentrate instead on making progress in working on each of the four life areas.

Remember, it is an expression of your wholeness to be in touch with your past. It is not at all a bad thing to think back over both the good and bad aspects of your life. Often it is a sign of respect or affection that people and events are remembered, either with laughter or with tears.

Even those events that cannot be remembered without a twinge of pain, and that seem to have much more evil than good associated with them, simply reflect the fact that the event is still with you, that you have not denied it by blocking it out.

Far too often, people try to bury bad or unhappy experiences in the past, never to be remembered or talked about again, for fear of having to relive traumatic and painful memories. The result is that these people end up spending a great deal of energy holding unwanted thoughts and feelings in check. It is like trying to hold balloons underwater. You might be able to hold a bunch of balloons underwater pretty easily — for a while. But, before long, you discover that it takes an enormous amount of energy to keep those balloons below the surface. So much energy in fact, that you have very little left over for anything else.

To live in the present and the future following a crisis does not mean that you shut the whole thing completely out of awareness, forget it, or bury it in the past. Rather, it means that the event gradually becomes part of your personal history. It takes its place beside all the other experiences of your life, requiring less and less of your immediate attention and energy.

IF THE CRISIS WAS MANY YEARS AGO, ISN'T IT TOO LATE TO CHANGE?

Our view is that it is never too late to change — especially if you want to badly enough. Your motivation — that fierce inner drive or determination to change — makes all the difference.

Clinical work with people in crisis has shown that crises are times when a person is ripe for change. Since everything in life seems to have fallen apart, or is in jeopardy and unstable, people are often more ready to make needed changes than during times of calm and stability. This is why we have emphasized in this book that the prime time to begin change is in the immediate weeks and months following the crisis event. Of course, the change may not be completed until many months or years later — but in the first months after the crisis you will begin to put the changes in motion.

The problem with waiting too long after the crisis to begin making changes in your life is, as we have pointed out, that the equilibrium you regain — the new steady state — may be harmful to you in the long run. The pain becomes familiar — not comfortable or wanted, but familiar — and the familiar is difficult to give up.

Remember, however, that some other unsettling event down the line, many years after the previous crisis is over, can bring the original issues to the surface once more. This dredging-up process is like a mini-crisis. For some people the unsettling event may be nothing more than seeing a movie, or hearing a certain song, a sermon, or a conversation with a friend. Suddenly, for whatever reason, something has touched an exposed nerve. The pain starts again. Feelings that were never expressed start to come out. Haunting thoughts start haunting again. Gaping holes in relationships become apparent.

It could happen as you read this book. If you have an unresolved crisis in your past, then reading about a particular crisis experience and thinking back to your own might cause you to feel bad — guilty perhaps, because you have not done things "right" by the book.

If this describes your situation, treat this unwelcome recollection as a mini-crisis. You can then use the "four-bases" plan to rework the old crisis — *any* past crisis in your life. Think of your life since the crisis event and ask yourself, "What do I now need in order to face the future?"

Often you will find that the answer lies in something you have left out. Maybe it was some bit of information that was missing or perhaps the fact that a shattered belief was never replaced. Or it may be that some area of life — work, play, relationships — was never adequately rebuilt after the crisis. Whatever it is, now is the time to attend to it, to heal the hurt, and to grow.

WON'T TIME HEAL?

Yes, time often helps, but it can just as easily hurt. The passage of time, if not directed properly, can allow you to develop hurtful lifestyle patterns. A crisis cannot be healed or forgotten in a week or two, or a couple of months. Time does help to smooth the rough places out, but it needs your attention to the Four Tasks to heal fully. Real growth takes time, and also guided, determined effort. It usually doesn't happen by itself.

A FINAL WORD

You can apply the plan we've talked about in this book to your situation. People are doing it every day — people just like you who have suffered a crisis in one form or another. One very important and hope-giving aspect of this plan is that there are immediate gains along the way. Some of these gains may be small, but they are significant. And, one by one, as you work on some goal or accomplish some task, these gains will add up — eventually they'll add up to new life in a new world. These small successes will keep you going through the times when you feel like quitting, when things look bleak and discouragement crowds close.

There is danger in a crisis, yes. But it is our hope that we have shown you the opportunity present in the worst of situations. Hidden opportunity, perhaps, but present nonetheless. The plan for crisis resolution we have described in detail is designed to help you find that opportunity and make the most of it, to emerge from the crisis stronger, more self-assured, and far more resilient than you thought possible.

You don't have to just go through a crisis, you can *grow* through a crisis. Thousands of people have done it. You can, too.

• APPENDIX A •

Developmental Crises: Seasons of Change

SOME CRISES involve a struggle to move from one developmental stage to another. The outward signs of disorganization are actually a reflection of a normal maturational process. The transition can be fairly painless, like a sunny glide across a friendly lagoon; or it can more closely resemble a stormy North Sea crossing. Whether smooth and sunny, or dark and storm-tossed, largely depends on how a person is equipped in five essential areas: knowledge, skills, willingness to take risks, social supports, and physical supports. A lack in one or more of these areas can mean that a person will not be able to make the transition adequately and will move into the next stage unable to deal with the challenges ahead.

Lack of Information. A young girl who has been given no previous information about menstruation may experience a crisis at the onset of puberty.

Lack of Skill. A young man who comes to marriage with no previous experience in handling small children and no role model from which to learn may be in for a rude awakening at the birth of his first child. There are skills to be learned in taking care of infants and toddlers — everything from feeding and changing diapers, to managing money differently and dealing with a changed marital relationship.

Inability to Take Risks. Moving away from home to attend college in a distant city can be frightening at age eighteen. It is risky business to leave everything familiar — the support of family and friends, home-cooked meals, security — and strike out on one's own. For one unused to taking risks — such as might be learned through sports, challenges in school, or working at a part-time job — the challenge represented by taking charge of one's life can lead to a crisis.

Lack of Social Support. For many of the major developmental transitions, the support of family and friends and others can be critical in determining whether a particular transition becomes a crisis or not. A woman who leaves a career she has worked hard to develop in order to have a baby will find herself in need of support from others who have been through the same experience, who know what she is going through, who care about her and can offer emotional support. Lack of this kind of social support can interfere with the transition and adjustment to motherhood.

Lack of Physical Support. Lack of money can interfere with a person's ability to negotiate many of the major developmental transitions. The inability to buy clothing for children, or to get the car repaired, or to pay creditors will seriously impair one's ability to cope.

THE DEVELOPMENTAL TABLE

As a backdrop to understanding developmental crisis, the following table summarizes the various stages of human development. You may find it interesting to look yourself up on the table and see what is "normal" for a person like you to be dealing with.

Remember, however, that no one fits the table perfectly. Unique personal characteristics, family life, education, particular experiences mean that no individual will fit a table like this precisely. At the same time, it presents common themes helpful in understanding predictable transitions that have crisis potential.

Notice that the table has four columns. The first lists the stage and the age range that accompanies it. The second column lists the transition theme common to that stage; this is followed by the tasks or preoccupations characteristic of this stage in the third column. The fourth column lists possible crisis events that could make the transition from one stage to another difficult.

Reading Between the Lines

In studying the developmental table you may find a general description of the crisis you are undergoing or recognize one from your past. You may, however, have to do some "reading between the lines" to discover the cause of your crisis.

Look at the crisis event (extramarital affair, fight between parent and child, an unwanted pregnancy, etc.) and ask yourself: does this event relate to any of the developmental issues listed under the "Tasks/Preoccupations" column of the table for my age group?

In other words, crises often arise when there are developmental issues present, but these issues are often below the surface. The fighting, the pregnancy, the affair, or whatever, diverts attention from the main issue — the developmental issue. Once you understand that there is a developmental issue being worked out you can begin to deal with it, giving as much attention to it as to the surface symptom.

Then, look more closely at the "Tasks/Preoccupations" related to the symptoms you are experiencing. Ask yourself if you are making progress in working out these tasks.

For example, if you were experiencing a crisis during the "Maturity" stage (ages fifty to sixty-five) you would want to ask yourself: Am I adjusting to the physical changes in my body that correspond to my age group? Have I made adequate preparation for retirement? How well am I developing adult relationships with my grown children?

A deficit in one of these areas might be the underlying cause of the crisis. Take it one step further and ask yourself: Am I having difficulty here because of a lack of one or more of the five personal resources described earlier — information, skill, physical or social support, risk taking? If so, what needs to be done? Do I need to develop some new skill? Or, do I need extra social support to help me take risks? Do I need somebody to help me sort through the whole thing?

This kind of self-questioning can deliver powerful results. By considering the themes and preoccupations of the table, you can begin to gain insight into the nature of your own crisis and begin laying the proper groundwork for growth.

STAGES OF HUMAN DEVELOPMENT

Stage	Transition Theme	Tasks/Preoccupations	Possible Crisis Events
Infancy (0–1)	Trust versus mistrust	Feeding Developing sensory discrimination and motor skills Gaining emotional stability	Disruption in feeding Physical illness, injury Rejection by primary caregiver
Toddlerhood (1–2)	Autonomy versus shame and doubt	Walking, talking Developing sense of independence Adjusting to socialization demands	Physical injury Conflict with primary caregiver over increased assertiveness, toilet training, etc.
Early Childhood (2–6)	Initiative versus guilt	Learning skills and muscle control Developing body concepts, and learning about sex differences Learning cultural values and sense of "right and wrong" Developing concepts of social and physical reality Developing interpersonal skills (family, peers)	Physical injury Conflict with teachers/parents re: early sex play Conflict with teachers, peers Entering school (preschool or kindergarten) Loss of friends through moving/migration

Stage	Transition Theme	Tasks/Preoccupations	Possible Crisis Events
Middle Childhood (6–12)	Industry versus inferiority	Mastering school subjects (three Rs, science, humanities)	Learning difficulties in school
		Developing learning and problem-solving skills	Peer conflicts
		Relating to peers, teachers, and unfamiliar adults	Conflict with teachers
		Developing sense of independence within family context	Conflict with parents
		Developing self-control and frustration tolerance	Change in schools
Adolescence (12–18)	Identity versus role confusion	Adjusting to bodily changes and new emotions	Menstruation
			Sexual intercourse
			Unwanted pregnancy
		Achieving gradual independence from parents/caretakers	Graduation from high school
		Questioning values/developing life philosophy	Going to college
			Conflict with parents over personal habits and lifestyle
		Exploring intimate personal relationships	Breakup with girl/boyfriend; broken engagement
		Exploring vocational options	Career indecision
			Difficulty on first job
			Success/failure in: academics, athletics

Young Adulthood (18–34)	Intimacy versus isolation	Selecting and learning to live with a mate/partner	Rejection by potential partner; extramarital affairs; separation, divorce
		Starting a family (or, not . . .)	Unwanted pregnancy; inability to bear children; birth of a child
		Developing parenting skills	Discipline problems with children; illness of son or daughter; inability to manage the various demands of parental role
		Deciding about military service	Entering military service; being drafted, avoiding service
		Getting started in an occupation	Academic difficulties; failure to graduate from high school/college; inability to find satisfactory career; poor performance in chosen career
		Overall development of personal lifestyle in social context	Purchase of home; financial difficulties; conflict between career and family goals; age-30 transition

Stage	Transition Theme	Tasks/Preoccupations	Possible Crisis Events
Middle Adulthood (35–50)	Generativity versus stagnation	Adjusting to physiological changes of middle age	Awareness of physical decline
			Chronic illness (self or spouse)
			Climacteric
		Adjusting to changes in children (e.g., to young adults)	Rejection by rebellious adolescent children
			Divorce of child
		Dealing with new responsibilities regarding aging parents	Decision about care of aging parents
			Death or prolonged illness of parents
		Increasing productivity and developing socioeconomic consolidation	Setback in career; conflict at work
			Financial concerns
			Moving associated with career advancement
			Unemployment
		Re-examination of earlier life choices (mate, career, children) and reworking of earlier themes (identity; intimacy)	Awareness of discrepancy between life goals and achievements
			Regret over earlier decision not to marry, not to have children, or vice versa
			Dissatisfaction with goals achieved

Stage	Psychosocial crisis	Developmental tasks	Events/Stressors
		Shift in life structure in light of changes in family and work responsibilities	Promotion Break/conflict with mentor Marital problems/extramarital affairs Return to work (female), post-childrearing Death of friend(s)
Later Adulthood (50–65)	Generativity versus stagnation	Adjusting to physiological aging (e.g., changes in health, decreased strength) Preparing for retirement	Health problems Decisions re: retirement (leisure time, new career) Change in physical living arrangements (farmhouse to city apartment)
		Developing mutually rewarding relationships with grown children	Conflict with grown children "Empty nest" (last child leaves home)
		Re-evaluating, consolidating relationship with spouse/significant other, or adjusting to his/her loss (death, divorce)	Death of spouse, divorce
		Assisting aging parents Making productive use of increased leisure time	Conflict with parents Resistance to retirement (separation or letting go of work roles/responsibilities)

Stage	Transition Theme	Tasks/Preoccupations	Possible Crisis Events
Older Adulthood (65–death)	Ego integrity versus despair	Pursuing second/third career and/or leisure interests	Financial difficulties
		Sharing wisdom from life's experience with others	Interpersonal conflict with children
			Interpersonal conflict with peers (e.g., in new living quarters)
			Neglect by adult children
		Evaluating past and achieving sense of satisfaction with one's life	Death of friends
		Enjoying reasonable amount of physical and emotional comfort	Awareness of loneliness
		Maintaining sufficient mobility for variety in environment	Illness or disability
			Difficulty in adjustment to retirement

Situational Crises: When Bad Things Happen

WHILE SOME crises can be traced to problems in normal human development, others are completely unpredictable, occurring as a result of some unexpected event in a person's life. The loss of home and family through a natural disaster, terminal illness, rape, being held hostage under threat of death — events such as these can cause *situational* crises.

In a situational crisis there is little or no association between the crisis and the person's age or stage of development. These crises can strike anyone, at any time — which means few people are prepared for or believe that situational crises will happen to them. Most people tend to believe that serious injury, getting fired, premature death of a loved one, and so on happen only to the "other guy."

THE MAKING OF A CRISIS

The table of Situational Crises lists the most common types of situational crises. As you look at the list, remember that not every traumatic event that befalls a person leads to crisis. Whether an event or experience becomes a crisis depends upon one or more of the following factors:

The event represents a loss. The loss could be physical, as in the loss of a loved one through death, or psychological as in the loss of a life's dream or the loss of self-esteem or security. A concert violinist who loses the use of his hands through arthritis has lost more than a livelihood; he may perceive that he has lost his vision for life, his goals, his self-respect, his identity.

The event presents an obstacle to a life's goal. The event may present what seems like an insurmountable obstacle to moving into the future according to one's plans. If a fourth-year medical student is kicked out of school or a corporate executive is fired from her job, such an event might lead to crisis for either of these individuals since basic life goals have been blocked in each case.

The event taxes limited resources. Whenever a person is ill-equipped to deal with a certain event — whether of a catastrophic nature or relatively benign — the potential for crisis is present. During any time of stress, the personal resources of knowledge, skill, ability to take risks, physical and social support are drawn upon in one way or another. If these resources are low or nonexistent, a crisis might well ensue. A bank failure, for instance, could well bring about a crisis for a pensioner whose life savings were tied up in a ruined savings account, while it would merely represent a momentary vexation for a wealthy individual.

The event touches off unfinished business. Sometimes an event may seem innocent on the surface yet represent some aspect of the past that a person has neglected or avoided dealing with. A move to a new city could become a crisis for a person who has never faced isolation or loneliness. In the same way, not getting a certain job could produce a crisis for someone who had never learned how to deal with setbacks.

The presence of any one or more of these factors could signal a crisis when combined with one of the situations from the following table.

SITUATIONAL CRISES

General Category	Possible Crisis Events
Physical injury/illness (and other health-related crises)	Admission to or discharge from a hospital Drug problem (dependency, etc.) Surgery Loss of a limb Stroke Diagnosis of cancer or other life-threatening illness Physical disability or other permanent injury
Unexpected death	Fatal accident Fatal disease Homicide Suicide
Crime: victims and offenders	Victim of robbery Victim of physical assault Arrest for offense (e.g., driving while intoxicated) Indictment for criminal activity Incarceration
Natural and manmade disasters	Loss due to tornado, hurricane, fire, flood, etc. Threat to health from discovery of buried chemical wastes Loss from airline crash Danger resulting from nuclear accident (e.g., Three-Mile Island)

General Category	Possible Crisis Events
War and related acts	Induction into the armed services
	Discharge from armed services (e.g., return home after foreign military service)
	Combat trauma (Post-Traumatic Stress Disorder)
Job-related crises	Demotion
	Political "backstabbing"
	Promotion (or absence of promotion)
Financial crises	Loss of job
	Financial setback due to poor investments
	Conflict with creditors
	Bankruptcy
Divorce/separation	Marital conflict leading to divorce
	Dispute over financial settlement, custody of/access to children
Family crises	Marital infidelity
	Marital fight (physical or verbal)
	Child abuse
	Spouse battering
	Academic difficulty of children
	Discipline problem with child, at home or in school
Migration (moving to a new community)	Conflict between parents (and children) over whether to move to a new community
	Leaving friends and loved ones behind; coping with stress of the moving process
	Adjustment to a new community

• APPENDIX C •

Getting Outside Help:
A Consumer's Guide

THROUGHOUT THIS BOOK we have emphasized the importance of using all your available resources during periods of extreme upset. Friends, co-workers, clergy, physicians, lawyers, counselors, and others can often make a critical contribution to the healing process.

This appendix is an introduction to some of the standard resources available in your own community — specifically, the psychological and counseling services that may be helpful to you in working through a crisis — and can serve as a guide to getting outside help.

What Kind of Outside Help Might I Need?
Depending upon the areas of your life that have been most severely affected by the crisis, you may find, in the immediate days and weeks following a crisis event, that you need one or more of the following:
— money
— food
— shelter
— legal advice
— medical assistance
— someone to talk to

— employment
— transportation
— child care

Most communities offer a wide range of social services in these and other areas. Many of these services come from the private sector, while others are available to you through public agencies, churches, hospitals, or other helping organizations.

How Do I Find Out About These Services?

You have two avenues open to you. The first is your own existing network of friends and acquaintances — ask those you know what services they are aware of. If a friend was helped by a certain therapist in a time of crisis, chances are you will be able to establish rapport with that person fairly quickly. Start with friends and acquaintances you know; ask them to refer you to people they trust.

The second approach is to go directly to the public agencies themselves. Sit down at the telephone with paper and pencil and begin making phone calls, looking for information. There are several ways to begin:

• *United Way.* The United Way office in every community keeps a list of agencies and individuals who provide helping services in your community and can put you in touch with the proper services.

• *Hot lines and information services.* Look in your phone book, or call the operator to ask for crisis hot lines in your community. They go under a variety of names: Problems of Living Lines, Crisis Lines, Help Lines, or Information and Referral Services. The one thing they all have in common is that they are staffed by trained volunteers who have handled crises of every description and are good at putting people in touch with community resources. They all maintain comprehensive lists of phone numbers and addresses of helping agencies available in or near your community. Use these people — it only takes a phone call.

• *Yellow Pages.* The Yellow Pages of the phone book are becoming more and more specific each year. Therefore, start looking under the heading of the kind of help you require — marital, legal, medical, et cetera. You'll find the numbers of all kinds of services, so this is more chancy than asking someone you know, but it's a start.

What Happens After I Get Someone on the Phone?

From the very beginning think of yourself as a consumer of a service. This means you have a right to ask questions before giving your time, energy, and money to anyone offering professional assistance.

If the receptionist can answer all your questions, great! If not, politely ask to speak to someone else who might know more about the particular service you're requesting. The following are entirely appropriate questions to ask over the phone:

• What services do you provide?
• How much will it cost? Do you have a sliding scale? Must I pay right away, or will you bill me? Will my insurance cover the service?
• Will I have a specific appointment?
• May I come during my lunch hour, or in the evening, or on Saturday?
• How long a wait will there be once I get there?
• Are your records confidential?

In other words, get as much information as you can over the phone, and don't be afraid to ask questions.

How Do I Know if I Need Professional Counseling?

In most cases, you will not need a professional counselor to weather a crisis. By using the principles outlined in this book, you will be able to work through the crisis on your own, at your own speed. But there may be times when the crisis seems to dwarf any attempt to resolve it, or when you find yourself stuck.

Professional counseling help may be needed if:

— After a period of months (or years) following the crisis event, you find yourself closed to the prospect of living a full life.

— The crisis event is seriously interfering in one or more of the behavioral areas necessary to living a full life — work, play, relationships, physical health.

— In the weeks and months following the crisis event, you are having extreme difficulty applying the principles outlined in this book.

Beyond these general guidelines, if you feel suicidal or are afraid you might hurt someone else, don't delay in getting outside help. Allow a professional counselor to provide support and help you through the pain and confusion.

How Much Will Counseling Cost?

Since psychotherapy and counseling are services, you usually pay an hourly rate. This rate, however, can range anywhere from free to $100 or more per hour. Many therapists and clinics have a sliding scale that sets the fee according to an individual's or family's ability to pay. Ask about this when you call.

Health insurance will often pay for psychotherapy, depending on the policy and the type of coverage involved. Also, prepaid health plans sometimes offer a wide range of psychotherapeutic services through Health Maintenance Organizations (HMOs). It may be that you are covered for the help you need. Check your policy to make sure, or call your insurance company to find out.

If you have insurance through your employer and are worried about your employer's finding out that you are receiving psychological services, call the insurance company directly and ask them how to get around this. You can probably send your claim directly to the insurance company and by-pass your own employer.

Aren't All Counselors Pretty Much Alike?

No. Although people have been offering help to other people for centuries, the formal helping professions — with labels, degrees, credentials, and so on — are a twentieth-century phenomenon. A glance in any phone book under the headings of "Marriage and Family Counseling" or "Psychotherapy" will reveal a full range of professional helpers — often with widely differing training, methods, and specialties.

One difference between therapists is professional training. A psychologist has a doctor of philosophy degree (Ph.D.) in psychology, while a psychiatrist has a medical doctor's degree (M.D.). This means that they have had different course work and likely have different specialties. At the same time, there may have been considerable overlap in skills and training. Psychologists, psychiatrists, social workers, psychiatric nurses, and pastoral counselors may all draw on similar psychotherapeutic approaches.

In choosing a counselor, inquire about credentials — that is, professional degrees and affiliations within the counselor's specialty (psychiatry, social work, and so on). Does he have a license? Is she listed with the National Register of Health Service Providers in Psychology? Is he affiliated with the Academy of Certified Social Workers?

While certification and licensure do not guarantee competence, they do indicate that the therapist is responsible to a group of peers charged with monitoring professional practice and receiving complaints.

Beyond special credentials and recognized professional affiliations, your main concern should be that the counselor is experienced in dealing with the problems you are facing. Find out if the therapist has helped people with divorce, death, physical injury, or whatever your situation may be.

How Can I Find a Therapist Who Might Be Good for Me?

While the Yellow Pages of your phone book may be a place to start, a better approach might be to ask your physician, lawyer, or minister — someone you know who is also concerned with helping others.

Because it's fairly common for people to come to their pastor or physician with psychological problems, these professionals are in the habit of referring clients who need help in special circumstances. Physicians, pastors, and lawyers have a special interest in knowing the names of good, qualified counselors because they do not want to send their own patients and clients to people who are not reputable or effective.

No matter who refers you, it is still important to ask your own questions about treatment. Do not allow a personal recommendation to take the place of asking your own questions or voicing your own concerns. Every individual is different and has different needs; a referral is no guarantee you will like the therapist. You must satisfy yourself the counselor is right for you.

Selecting a therapist is a very personal matter. In all probability you won't make much progress in therapy unless you feel comfortable talking with the counselor you select. Therefore, let your own personal reaction be the acid test. Ask yourself: "Do I feel I can open up to this person? Even though I may be nervous about starting, do I sense that this is a person who can help me?"

If the answer to these questions is yes, then get started. If you answered no, keep looking. There are good people available in every community; stay with the search until you find a good match between your needs and the help a counselor has to offer.

Most of life's traumas will not require the help of a professional to get you through. But when outside help is needed, do not hesitate to ask. There is no stigma in asking for help when it is necessary, and, used wisely, it could save you a lot of pain and hardship in the long run. Talking to a professional could be your smartest move.

Bibliography

Auerbach, S. M., and P. R. Kilmann. "Crisis Intervention: A Review of Outcome Research." *Psychological Bulletin* 84 (1977): 1189–1217.

Beck, A. T. "Cognition, Affect, and Psychopathology." *Archives of General Psychiatry* 24 (1971): 495–500.

Buchholz, D., and E.F.L. Niedermeyer. "Sleep Disorders." In *The Principles and Practice of Medicine,* edited by A. M. Harvey et al., 21st edition. Norwalk, Conn.: Appleton-Century-Crofts, 1984.

*Colgrove, M., H. Bloomfield, and P. McWilliams. *How to Survive the Loss of a Love.* New York: Bantam, 1976.
A truly supportive and realistic book on working through the loss of any relationship.

*Cooper, K. H. *The New Aerobics.* New York: Bantam, 1970.
On getting started in aerobic exercise, by the founding father.

*Cousins, N. *Anatomy of an Illness.* New York: Bantam, 1979.
A classic by the man who "laughed himself well," on the relationship between emotional and physical well-being.

*Ellis, A., and R. A. Harper. *A New Guide to Rational Living.* Englewood Cliffs, N.J.: Prentice-Hall, 1975.
A classic book on the relationship between thoughts, feelings, and behavior.

Fry, W. F. "Laughter and Health." In *Encyclopaedia Britannica's Annual Medical and Health Supplement for 1984,* edited by E. Bernstein, 259–62. Chicago: Encyclopedia Britannica, 1984.

*For further reading.

————. "The Psychobiology of Humor." Address given at Salt Lake City Conference on the Psychobiology of Health and Healing, sponsored by Brigham Young University, Provo, Utah, February 1982.

*Goldberg, H. *The New Male: From Self-Destruction to Self-Care.* New York: Signet, 1979.
An engrossing book, helpful for both men and women who want to improve the quality of adult intimacy.

Guest, J. *Ordinary People.* New York: Viking Press, 1976.

Hammond, D. C., and K. Stanfield. *Multidimensional Psychotherapy: A Counselor's Guide for the MAP Form.* Champaign, Ill.: Institute for Personality and Ability Testing, 1977.

*Hittleman, R. L. *Introduction to Yoga.* New York: Bantam Books, Inc., 1980.
An introduction to yoga as a method for relaxation and increased physical well-being.

Holmes, T. H., and R. H. Rahe. "The Social Readjustment Rating Scale." *Journal of Psychosomatic Research* 11 (1967): 213–18.

Horowitz, M. J. "Diagnosis and Treatment of Stress Response Syndromes: General Principles." In *Emergency and Disaster Management: A Mental Health Sourcebook,* edited by H. J. Parad, H.L.P. Resnik, and L. G. Parad. Bowie, Md.: The Charles Press Publishers, 1976.

*Jacobson, E. *Progressive Relaxation.* Chicago: University of Chicago Press, Midway Reprint, 1974.
Step-by-step descriptions of deep-muscle relaxation techniques used in behavior therapy.

*Kushner, H. S. *When Bad Things Happen to Good People.* New York: Schocken Books, 1981.
A rabbi's guide for gaining mental and spiritual mastery over life's tragedies.

Lazarus, A. A., ed. *Multimodal Behavior Therapy.* New York: Springer Publishing Co., 1976.

————. *The Practice of Multimodal Therapy.* New York: McGraw-Hill, 1981.

*For further reading.

Lazarus, R. S. "The Stress and Coping Paradigm." In *Competence and Coping During Adulthood,* edited by L. A. Bond and R. C. Rosen. Hanover, N.H.: University Press of New England, 1980.

*Lewis, C. S. *A Grief Observed.* New York: Seabury Press, 1961.
The author's personal walk through the intense grief following the death of his wife.

Mayer, N. *The Male Mid-Life Crisis: Fresh Starts After Forty.* New York: Doubleday, 1978.

Neugarten, B. L. "Time, Age, and the Life Cycle." *The American Journal of Psychiatry* 136 (1979): 887–93.

Selye, H. *The Stress of Life.* New York: McGraw-Hill, 1976.

*Sheehy, G. *Passages.* New York: E. P. Dutton, 1976.
A popular description of predictable crises of adult life; includes summaries of developmental psychology research on the topic.

*Simonton, C., S. Matthews-Simonton, and J. Creighton. *Getting Well Again.* Los Angeles: J. P. Tarcher, 1978.
A profound description of the relationship between psychological and physical well-being, with descriptions of techniques used to aid cancer victims.

*Slaikeu, K. A. *Crisis Intervention: A Handbook for Practice and Research.* Boston: Allyn and Bacon, 1984.
A comprehensive summary of crisis theory, an intervention model, and chapters on crisis intervention by police, clergy, teachers, counselors, health professionals, and employers.

Taylor, S. E. "Adjustment to Threatening Events: A Theory of Cognitive Adaptation." *American Psychologist* 38 (1983): 1161–73.

*Woolfolk, R. L., and F. C. Richardson. *Stress, Sanity, and Survival.* New York: Monarch, 1978.
An excellent summary of psychologically based stress management techniques.

*For further reading.